Praise for *You Can't Make This Stuff Up*

❝ With an apologetic grin to Lady Justice and the touch of a convincing closing argument, Gregg Naclerio tells readers the truth about a criminal justice world of miscommunications, misidentifications, misunderstandings, misdirections, and misadventures, proving beyond a reasonable doubt that behind every great criminal law war story is a lawyer with a sense of humor.❞

— **Landis Wade**, *recovering North Carolina trial lawyer, host of*
Charlotte Readers Podcast, *and author of*
The Christmas Courtroom Trilogy

❝ As a former law enforcement official who enjoys a friendship with Gregg, I have waited with great excitement for this chronicle of his experiences. His legal acumen, his keenly honed sense of humor, and his compassion make this a book to be enjoyed and not easily forgotten.❞

— **Det. Lt. Edith J. Platt**, *Massachuesetts State Police, retired*

❝ Grab your glass and put your feet up. The stories you are about to read are real and well told; some may warm your heart, others confound, but most will make you smile.

Forget TV, these are real and true recollections of the author's encounters with clients, police, the medical community, and the courts. Each one takes us into a moment in a person's life that most of us would hope to avoid.

Author Gregg Naclerio takes us inside and shows us ordinary people as their lives are upended. The outcomes can be seen as positive or negative, shaded by point of view. Naclerio shows how the system, when administered by professional, caring people, can turn near tragedy into recovery, and restore justice for all.

— **Barbara Shavelson**, *retired administrator, lover of good books*

" Knowing my friend Gregg Naclario, it is easy to picture him in the funny but true stories he tells the reader. I hear his voice and see his face as each story is told. It was good to read in these stories that police officers and lawyers like Gregg did what was needed at the time for the people they were hired to serve.

I was discussing the title of this book with another friend who is a federal probation officer. A big smile came across his face and his eyes got bright. He started telling me similar stories that he has seen while in court. Yes, the court system we still have today can be a funny place to work."

– **Reed Jones**, *former police officer, retired business man, community volunteer, woodworker*

" I practiced law in New York City for over 40 years. I was an assistant district attorney in the Brooklyn DA's office for eight years and took 75 jury verdicts. The next 35 years were spent in private practice predominately on the civil side, taking another 80 jury verdicts. I can tell you that this book gives you not only factual information about that goes into the daily life of a trial attorney; it also gives you the emotional and sometimes out of body experience of a trial attorney. In one story, during jury deliberations, Gregg relates a conversation he had with the detective who arrested his client about the New York Mets. The only way a trial attorney can survive is to sometimes detach from the emotional strain that he or she is under during a trial. This book not only tells you what transpires but how it feels to experience the day-to-day activities of a trial attorney. You Can't Make This Stuff Up is the kind of book you won't want to put down."

– **Robert M. Spadaro**, *Esquire*

" I'll begin by saying I love the title, You Can't Make This Stuff Up. The title alone suggests the reader is about to read content that is unusual, exciting and true. This book satisfied all of my senses. It made me sad, made me laugh and had me at the edge of my seat rushing to reach the end of each story. This book truly gives the reader insight into the world of law, the lives of attorneys and judges and the lives of people who commit crimes all.

I felt I was there watching the scene in person. I could see myself in the courtroom as the trials unfold, in the client meetings, in the strategy sessions. I enjoyed the nonchalant and simple explanations of the legal terms. The author's explanations left no guess work as to what was being talked about.

One of my favorite parts of this book is the reference to the Dice of Life lecture delivered by a judge. It was a true "made you think" moment. "

– Natalie Garfield

" I absolutely loved reading *You Can't Make This Stuff Up*. Gregg's writing style and storytelling are nothing short of authors like Child, Patterson, Baldacci, or Woods. When he describes any character in one of his "war stories," the reader can see that person in his or her mind. And just to bring it into focus, he will throw out a reference such as "Yogi Berra lookalike" or "Laurel and Hardy fit the duo" or "Kenna resembled Beyoncé." He inserts current events to put things into perspective, draw the reader in and make them a part of the story.

I enjoyed reading the book and anxiously await the opportunity to purchase a second book should Gregg decide to write another one."

– N.K. Harper, *retired police officer*

To Matt
Best of Luck
on your legal career.
It's the Best
Job in the
World

YOU CAN'T MAKE THIS STUFF UP

MY CRIMINAL LAW WAR STORIES

Enjoy the Book!
Hook 'em Horns

GREGG NACLERIO

6·30·21

LYSTRA BOOKS
& Literary Services

Fifty percent of the profit of this book will be donated to the Citizens Assisting Police Christmas gift program for needy children and Nourishing Noggins, which provides food and other basic necessities to students in need. Both are based in Cary, North Carolina.

You Can't Make This Stuff Up: My Criminal Law War Stories
Copyright © 2021 by Gregg Naclerio
All rights reserved

ISBN paperback 978-1-7363055-1-5
ISBN ebook 978-1-7363055-2-2
Library of Congress Control Number: 2021905671

Book design by Kelly Prelipp Lojk

Author's photo by Barbara Lynn

LYSTRA BOOKS
& Literary Services

Published by Lystra Books & Literary Services, LLC
391 Lystra Estates Drive, Chapel Hill, NC 27517
lystrabooks@gmail.com

This book is dedicated...

To those who helped me be the person I am: my father, Joe; mother, Gloria; uncles John and Mario; the fiery redhead of the family, Aunt Chippy; Frank Bianchino; Tony Bonaparte and Tony Scuderi.

To those who taught me how to be a trial attorney: Jeff Sorge, Pat Matthews, Frank Vergata, Rick Ellman, Bob Sale, Peter Yellin, Frank Yanelli, Jimmy LaRosa, Ben Brafman, Mel Ruskin and Judges John Copertino and Marie Santagata.

To all those who helped me on this journey, especially my wife of over fifty years, Charleen, who not only supported us when I was in law school but supported me when I doubted myself, and to my daughter, Barbara, who grew up to be a special lady even when I was too busy to be there as much as I should have.

And to my former colleagues at the Nassau County Legal Aid Society, the Special Prosecutors Office for Medicaid Fraud Control, and Ruskin Moscou Faltischek, PC.

Contents

Preface

Hey, glad you could make it. We are going to start very soon. Just remember that most trial attorneys don't like telling their war stories to civilians. You're invisible, so just sit there, listen in and make no noise.

A few minutes after you have been seated, Frank and Patrick, criminal law trial attorneys who have been my friends for years, meet me at the Caucus Bar for after-work cocktails. When such a group convenes—usually in the presence of beer for the Irish or Scotch for the rest of us— the conversation inevitably turns to the sharing of war stories. I told my share of stories, and I listened and absorbed the stories of other people. Some memories are sad, some funny and some just downright unbelievable, yet all of us who shared in the combat of practicing criminal law have their stories. What follows are mine.

My stories are true accounts of events based upon my personal experience or my conversations with individuals actively involved in the reported events.

Of course, I had to use some literary license to convey the feelings I experienced and to share them with you, because real life is not just a recitation of facts but also the emotions that accompany them.

Yes, I am sure I forgot some of the specific facts of each case and had to make some things up to have the tales flow. Let's say my stories are semi-true. And isn't that true enough?

For me, that is the key to this book. The stories are real to me because I lived them. Most people just see the beginning and/or the end of a criminal case as presented in the press or on TV. My stories will take you through a case from start to finish. You'll get to see and appreciate what happens in those key moments from crime and arrest to a jury's verdict. You'll see the process that makes me proud to be a lawyer.

As we peel back the cover of a criminal case, you'll see how real people—police officers, lawyers, judges, witnesses, defendants and their family members—deal with real-life situations. If I have done my job correctly, you'll be able to feel and share in their hopes, joys, sadness, successes and failures. As I look back on these cases, I feel it was a privilege to work with so many good and caring people, and I am proud to introduce you to them.

Even though most of these cases received attention in the local press, all the names of the individuals involved, as well as some of the fact patterns, have been changed to protect their privacy or that of their families, as many of these individuals have gone from this life. Additionally, the quotes I use are true representations of conversations and transcripts but may not be verbatim reporting.

The idea for this book came to me when I read the words chiseled into the west facade of the Nassau County courthouse located at 262 Old Country Road in Mineola, New York: JUSTICE IS GOD'S IDEA—MAN'S IDEAL.

I first saw these words in 1972 as a newly minted attorney working for the Nassau County Legal Aid Society. Later in my career, I would see those words as a special assistant attorney general prosecuting Medicaid fraud cases, and still later as a criminal defense attorney at Ruskin Moscou Faltischek, a prominent Long Island law firm. In my forty-year-plus legal career, I observed police officers, prosecutors, defense counsel and judges try to reach the ideal of justice. In the pursuit of justice, events unfolded both in and out of the courtroom that were bizarre and not reported to the public. When one of these events occurred, a colleague would say: "That's one for the book we should write." That was as far as we got. Until now.

So buckle up your seatbelts, make sure your seat back tray table is in its full upright and locked position, because I am going to take you on a flight to discover what it's *really* like to practice criminal law.

You Haven't Lived
Until You've Seen a Pan of Lasagna
Smashed Against a Wall

When she first called 911, she was afraid *of* him; now, she was afraid *for* him.

Nina Bearachi was preparing the family an early lunch when she asked her husband, Benedict, why he had stopped taking his medication. When he ignored her question, she pressed the issue.

"The doctor told you, you need to take your pills twice a day, and you haven't for the last two days."

Nina's rebuke caused Benedict, seated at the head of the table, to jump to his feet, grab the table in his large, strong hands and flip it. The plates, utensils and glassware smashed and scattered over Nina's once pristine floor. When she yelled at him, Benedict bolted to their bedroom and returned with his hunting rifle.

As he chambered a round into the rifle, he screamed, "Shut the hell up or I'll make sure you never say another word."

Nina grabbed her two young daughters and ran out of her home. From the safety of her neighbors' home across the street, Nina called 911. Soon, a uniformed Nassau County patrolman pulled his cruiser up to the house she and her husband worked so hard to afford. Nina saw Officer John Gugliamenti walk up the five steps to the front door and knock on it. Benedict opened the door. He and the officer were separated only by a screen door. Nina saw the officer raise both hands above his head and slowly back down the steps. It was then that Nina realized Benedict was pointing the rifle at the officer.

When Gugliamenti reached the bottom of the steps, he turned and ran in a zigzag pattern back to his squad car. Once he was safe in the car, Officer Gugliamenti called dispatch and requested back up.

Soon, Nina heard the sound of sirens coming down Hempstead Turnpike. Now they frightened her. Her fear had changed from being for herself and the girls to being for Benedict.

Officer Gugliamenti was not so conflicted.

A man with a gun always got a lot of attention, and Nassau County's elite crime prevention unit was on the way.

Within eight minutes of the patrolman's call, seven squad cars descended upon 47 Padre Road. Patrol cars blocked each intersection, and a perimeter was set up. Residences on both sides of the house were evacuated. Yellow police tape cordoned off the area as police officers crouched behind their squad cars and trained their .38-caliber Smith & Wesson service revolvers on the front door of the Bearachi home.

A uniformed sergeant with a bullhorn made his way to the police cruiser closest to the front of the residence to try and reason with Benedict.

"Mr. Bearachi, my name is Sergeant Mike Rice. Your home is surrounded by the police. We don't want to hurt you. Your wife Nina told me about you, that you are a good man. So please do the right thing and come out with your hands up. Nina and I want to help you. Please, come out, Mr. Bearachi."

The front door slammed shut. The siege of Padre Road had begun.

After this burst of police activity, the street became eerily quiet. The police hunkered down, waiting for the house's occupant to make the first move. The strobe lights of the police cruisers pierced the overcast sky, and the ominous arrival of an ambulance dispatched from the nearby Meadowbrook Hospital heightened the tense atmosphere.

All of these facts were included in the report Sergeant Rice radioed to police headquarters at 12:17 p.m. Just as Rice completed his radio report, he saw a man walking down the middle of the street like he was enjoying an early afternoon stroll. The man wore a New York Islander T-shirt and a pair of blue jeans. Rice was about to tell one of the officers to grab this lunatic and pull him out of harm's way when he saw the reflection of the strobe lights on the gold shield hanging on a lanyard around the man's neck. As the man got nearer, Rice recognized Detective Sergeant Wilson Kite, commander of the crime prevention unit's tactical team.

3

The CPU was created in the mid-sixties and was designed to target specific types of criminal conduct, mostly narcotics trafficking and high-risk tactical entries. Along with the precision firearms team and the crisis negotiators, they were Nassau's early version of today's SWAT team. The CPU's undercover officers were tough, seasoned cops who would do what they had to do to get the job done. The team took on the persona of its leader, who was known to be tough as steel, though he stood only five feet, six inches tall. Perhaps his nickname, "Wacky Wilson," said it all.

The first thing Wilson wanted to do was to speak to Nina. She told him that Benedict, who liked to be called Benny, was a good man, a hard worker and an attentive father. But on this day, he suffered from one of his now-all-too-frequent mood swings. Today, we probably would say Benny suffered from bipolar disorder, but whatever you wish to call it, the July 24, 1974, mood swing caused Benny to pick up his rifle and threaten his wife. Nina told Wilson that Benny was under the care of a psychiatrist but was refusing to take his prescribed medication. She insisted Benny was a sick man and not a criminal.

Such a statement brought little comfort to Detective Kite. He thought a sick man with a gun was perhaps even more dangerous than a hardened criminal with a gun. Criminals viewed arrests as a cost of doing business, and when the string ran out, they rarely took on the cops. A sick man was different. Would he blow his brains out, set the house ablaze or fire his rifle—and whatever other weapons he may have had—into the street indiscriminately? Those bullets could not only kill a police officer, but the ricocheting rounds could also strike one of the nosey neighbors, who were dividing their time between television news coverage of the US Supreme Court's unanimous decision that President Nixon must turn over the White House Watergate tapes to Special Prosecutor Leon Jaworski and peering out of their front windows at the local standoff. This situation was truly a powder keg. The only thing unknown was who would light the fuse.

Kite was a father himself, so he understood the words Nina spoke about Benny being a caring father who battled mental illness. Nevertheless, no matter how sympathetically Nina had painted him, Benny had to come out of the house of his own free will or be taken out forcefully.

The siege was now well into its fourth hour, and Benny still refused to speak to the police crisis negotiator or anyone else, for that matter. Neither the bullhorn shouts from the street nor their incessant calls to his home telephone brought any response from Benny.

The temperature approached ninety degrees, and the humidity was high. The police officers were getting impatient and restless. Kite decided to take a chance. He walked alone, past the ring of police cruisers directly in front of the house, and halfway up the lawn, toward Benny's front door. The detective called out to Benny. He got no response. Kite could see Benny standing in the living room window, looking quizzically back at him.

"Benny," Kite shouted, "all I want to do is talk to you." Still no response. Kite tried again.

"I'm taking off my gun, so you can trust me." Wilson Kite reached into his holster and threw his .357 Smith & Wesson revolver six feet away, onto the front lawn.

Several of the patrolmen circling the house uttered the

words, "He must be nuts." The CPU team members knew it was only one more instance of Wacky Wilson being Wacky Wilson. The CPU team also knew two things the other officers on scene did not. One, Kite was an expert in hand-to-hand combat, learning his craft compliments of the United States Marine Corps, and two, like every CPU officer, Kite carried a backup gun, a .38 snub-nosed pistol, tucked under his T-shirt in a holster clipped to his jeans at the small of his back. Although the situation was risky, they knew the boss could handle it.

At least they hoped so. A voice from inside the house yelled, "Sure." Kite had only walked another ten feet when the officers' hopes were dashed.

Benny appeared at the screen door and leveled the rifle at Kite, who by now stood a mere fifteen feet away. The next word from Benny really put fear into the hearts of the CPU team.

"Strip," Benny ordered. "You strip or you don't come in."

Kite had a split second to cycle through the options in his head. "Do I talk some more? Do I turn and leave? Would he shoot me in the back? Oh shit!"

What happened next was probably the first in the Nassau County Police Department. Kite kicked off his sneakers and took off his socks. When he removed his pants, he would have to make sure the .38 clipped to the back of his jeans was out of Benny's view. God only knew what a sick man with a gun might do if he felt betrayed.

With the skill of a surgeon, Kite opened his belt buckle and—hoping that the concealed gun would stay concealed—took off his pants. Thankfully, the holster remained clipped to his dungarees, and as soon as his pants were on the ground, his T-shirt followed, providing additional cover for the weapon. Now attired in his boxer shorts, the detective walked the remaining fifteen feet to the stoop and negotiated the five steps to the screen door, where Kite came face-to-face with Benny and the hunting rifle. The screen door opened, and Kite slowly disappeared into the house.

———

The moment Kite entered the house, tactical command of the situation reverted to Captain Barry Friedman, the department's watch commander located at police headquarters a few miles away in Mineola. The first order issued by Friedman led Lieutenant Christopher Monkart to climb onto the roof of the home directly across the street from Benny's.

Monkart was the CPU sniper. His orders were clear and succinct: "Observe, report, only fire to protect Kite."

Once on the roof, Monkart turned his baseball cap backwards and laid down on his old black yoga mat cut to fit his prone body and designed to protect him from the hot roof shingles. He loaded one round into the chamber of his Remington 700 P rifle, shut the bolt and steadied the weapon on its tripod. He used his telescopic sight to give him a close look inside 47 Padre Road.

Benny's house was about a hundred yards away from Monkart's perch. Next to the front door was a six-by-six-foot picture window.

Monkart reported to Captain Friedman that he could see Kite sitting on a couch that was pushed against the front wall, directly in front of the window. Monkart also reported that the suspect was about ten feet away from Kite with a rifle pointed in Kite's general direction. The suspect was speaking in an animated fashion that caused the rifle to bob up and down. Monkart also noted that the suspect had knocked over two side tables and a bookcase, so that a number of books were scattered over the living room floor.

Friedman told Monkart to continue to observe and report and confirmed that Monkart could take the shot if he believed it was necessary to save Kite's life. Monkart kept his finger on the trigger guard of his weapon and visualized the shot just as he had been trained to do. During his two tours of duty in Vietnam, he not only visualized many shots but also had taken several, all with lethal results. He knew what would happen if he had to squeeze the trigger. The chambered round would leave the rifle muzzle at a high velocity, shatter the front glass of the living room picture window, enter the target's skull, and shatter the glabella bone directly above and between the eyes before entering the prefrontal cortex of the brain, destroying the primary auditory cortex and cerebellum. Death would be instantaneous, and the target would not even hear the bang of the shot that killed him.

The sniper then reported to the watch commander that patrol officers were in position around the house and were equipped with a battering ram, ready to breech the house on command. Captain Friedman then directed Monkart and the breeching team to go to radio channel TAC 3. Friedman declared that, since Monkart had the best position to assess the tactical situation, the sniper had command authority to issue the order to breech the house, if needed. Minutes later, the other officers heard Monkart's first report.

"You won't believe this, but Kite is sitting on the couch, his back to the picture window, and he just stretched, putting his arms in the air as close to the window as possible, and both hands were showing the OK sign."

While none of the officers involved in the standoff expected Detective Kite and Benny to open the front door and walk out singing "Kumbaya," they all hoped—and some prayed—for a similar miracle.

When Kite first entered the house, Benny invited him to sit on the living room couch. It took some doing, as Kite had to maneuver the obstacle course of overturned furniture and books just to get to the couch. Fortunately, the back of the couch was pushed up against the large bay window and Kite knew someone would be watching his every movement and gesture. Benny had ripped the living room drapes off the picture window to give himself a clear shot at the police during the standoff. Now, the unobstructed view into the house not only worked to Kite's benefit but more importantly to Monkart's if he needed to take the shot.

So here was the scene: Detective Sergeant Wilson Kite of the Nassau County Police Department, in his boxer shorts, sat on a couch in Benny Bearachi's destroyed living room with Benny sitting ten feet away, occasionally pointing the hunting rifle at Kite's chest.

Although his outward demeanor appeared calm and, at times, even bored with Benny's rantings, Kite's mind was processing data like an IBM computer. Included in his calculations were:

Fact: Benny held a Savage 110 deer rifle with a detachable box magazine that could hold four .308 rounds.

Fact: The rifle was designed for hunting and was a powerful weapon that could take down a deer from seventy-five to a hundred yards.

Fact: The rifle was a bolt action model, which meant Benny had to manipulate the bolt in order to load a round into the chamber.

Fact: Assume there was a round already chambered and ready to be fired. After the first shot, Benny would need to pull back the bolt and feed the next round into the chamber. That would take time, and as soon as the officers outside heard a shot, Kite knew they would storm the living room.

Fact: The distance between Kite and the rifle was approximately ten feet, far too great for direct frontal attack.

Fact: Kite would only have one opportunity to take Benny down before he fired the rifle. He had better get it right or the alimony payments to his ex-wife would come to a screeching halt. (That thought made Kite smile, even if just in his mind.)

As he processed this information, and based upon his training, knowledge and skills, the detective came to the conclusion that the situation required he only take one action. Wait. For the time being, Kite sat back on the couch and waited like a cobra for his chance to strike.

As Benny pointed the rifle, sometimes to the floor and other times directly at him, Kite tried again to talk Benny into surrendering. Both men knew it was a useless conversation, but it was one that had to be had. After a while, Kite asked Benny to turn on the air conditioning since it was getting hotter in the house than it was outside. As a charming host would do, Benny started up the A/C system. Not only did Kite appreciate the cold air flowing, he knew the hum of the fan would help mask sounds his team would make if they began to break into the rear of the house for the take down.

Over the next hour, as their conversation turned to kids, wives, work and the heat wave, it did not take Kite long to realize that Nina was right—Benny was a sick man.

At times, Benny talked about being held prisoner in a World War II Japanese prison camp. That told Kite that Benny was delusional; he was in his late thirties and would have been a small child when the war ended. At other times, Benny told Kite that the medication his psychiatrist provided for him was poison, that the psychiatrist was having an affair with Nina and that she wanted him dead. "Dead" was not a word Kite wanted to hear or think about, since he was on the wrong end of a rifle.

After listening to Benny's delusions, the detective knew there was no way Benny would give up peacefully. It was now time to act, and acting was something Kite did very well.

"How about a drink?" Kite asked.

"What do you want?"

"A gin and tonic would be great. You can skip the lime," Kite responded.

"You can skip the tonic, too. We don't have any," Benny said, walking from the living room into the adjoining kitchen.

In the kitchen, Benny grabbed two glass tumblers, filled them halfway with ice and grabbed a bottle of no-name gin from the kitchen cabinet. Not wanting to alert Benny that this was a tactic to bring the two men closer together, Kite spread his arms over the back of the couch again, but this time, he did not give the OK sign. Monkart got the sense something was wrong and radioed a heads up to the breech team. Kite knew the attack had to work the first time because there probably would not be a second chance, especially if the rifle fired.

Kite took a deep breath, removed his hands from the back of the couch and put them on his knees. As Benny approached, trying to balance two glasses of ice, the bottle of gin and the long gun, the distance between the two men grew less and less—twenty feet, fifteen, ten, five. When Benny passed a glass to Kite, his rifle dipped to the floor. Wacky Wilson knew what to do.

The TAC 3 channel rang out with Monkart's order to the breech teams—"Go, go, go," when he saw Kite tackle Benny like a middle linebacker stacking up a halfback at the line of scrimmage.

As Kite hit Benny, the gin, ice, glasses and rifle flew into the air. Kite pinned Benny to the floor as the CPU team rushed into the house.

Benny was handcuffed and led out to a waiting police cruiser. Shortly thereafter, a uniformed officer, smiling from ear to ear, brought Kite's shirt, pants and two revolvers into the house. After five hours and thirty minutes, the siege at 47 Padre Road had ended.

No one had been hurt and Wacky Wilson was on his way to being named Police Officer of the Year.

———

Benny was calm and collected when he was led handcuffed into the Third Precinct to be photographed and fingerprinted. He cooperated by providing the squad with the necessary personal pedigree information required to complete the processing of an arrest. Subsequently, Benny's fingerprints were sent to the New York State Division of Criminal Justice Services in Albany so that a criminal record check could be performed and a NYSIS Record of Arrests and Prosecution document (commonly called a RAP sheet) could be obtained. Without the RAP sheet, a judge would not be able to set bail. Benny sat overnight in a detention cell and the following morning was transported to the district court, along with all the other people arrested the previous day. Handcuffed with two other prisoners, one on his right, the other on his left, Benny waited for his case to be called in arraignment court, then located at 400 County Seat Drive in Mineola.

———

When the case of *The People of the State of New York against Benedict G. Bearachi* was called, Benny, now known as the defendant, was brought before the judge. The judge advised Benny that he was charged with the felony of criminal possession of a weapon, a class D felony, and then gratuitously added that a conviction could result in a state prison term of seven years. When the judge heard the facts of Benny's standoff with the police, he ignored defense counsel's request for bail and ordered that a 730.30 exam be performed. The point of the exam was to ascertain if Benny had a mental disease or defect that resulted in him lacking the capacity, as the law states, "to understand the proceedings against him or assist in his defense." Accordingly, Benny was remanded to the Nassau County Correctional Center located less than two miles away from his home, for psychiatric testing.

Four weeks later, the court-appointed psychiatrist issued a report noting that Benny was competent to understand the charges against him and able to assist in his defense. The psychiatrist also stated that he had put Benny on a new medication, lithium, which was used to treat bipolar disorders; it counteracted both mania and depression. The doctor reported that Benny had responded well to the medication. Prior to the psychiatrist's report being submitted to the court, a grand jury indictment was filed that charged Benny with the felony of criminal possession of a weapon and the added misdemeanor charge of reckless endangerment.

It was at this time that the Legal Aid Society was formally assigned to represent Benny, and I became his lawyer.

It was the summer of 1974, and I had recently been promoted to the Nassau County Legal Aid Society's County Court Trial Bureau. It was a big step up for a lawyer barely two years out of school.

In district court, Legal Aid attorneys represented individuals charged with misdemeanors such as larceny, shoplifting, simple assault and drug possession. The maximum sentence a judge could impose was a term of one year. Experienced defendants referred to this sentence as a "bullet."

By contrast, the stakes for the defendants in county court were much higher. Conviction there could result in a sentence of many years to life in places located in upstate New York with such bucolic names as Attica, Green Haven, Dannemora, Fishkill and the Ossining Correctional Facility, affectionately known as Sing Sing.

Going to the county court trial bureau put a young lawyer like me in the big leagues in other ways as well. First, I got my own office, as opposed to sharing a two-room bullpen (which had been retrofitted out of a ladies restroom) with twelve other lawyers. I had my own secretary to share with only two other lawyers, and more importantly, I had the opportunity to work with, and learn from, the bureau's other lawyers who had years of experience trying cases.

I was able to try cases against the senior members of the district attorney's office. These assistant district attorneys were well-seasoned, and I had to be at the top of my game to avoid being embarrassed in court.

I also got the opportunity to meet and learn from the county's top criminal defense attorneys, who were never too busy to speak to me and share their insights on trial practice. Whenever I had time, I watched these attorneys in court. That was an education in and of itself.

Last, and by no means least, I obtained in-depth critical analysis of my trial practice skills by a group we called the Court Watchers. This group of several retired men made a daily pilgrimage to the courthouse and sat in on any of the trials in session. They were not bashful in telling my colleagues and me what we were doing right or wrong, based upon the insights they acquired by watching some of the best trial attorneys from New York City and the county. Just as important, they provided a view of the case from a juror's perspective, which was critical.

Becoming a criminal trial attorney meant learning on the job and was, in fact, largely self-taught. This is completely opposite from the training physicians receive. Once a person graduates medical school and receives a license to practice, the next step is an internship, followed by a residency program where teaching and learning continue for several years. On the other hand, any person who graduates law school and passes the bar exam is suddenly transformed into a lawyer who can go out and represent people on his or her own. A bit scary when I think about it.

In the Beginning

I graduated law school wanting to practice criminal law. However, my choice of jobs right out of school was limited to government service because only the top graduates from the top law schools got a chance to work in the criminal law departments at the large, so-called "white shoe" law firms. The practice of criminal law seems to work best in a solo practice or a small firm of three or four lawyers. Accordingly, there are not many places in the private sector where a first-year criminal lawyer can obtain a job.

My resume showed above-average academic achievements from Holy Cross High School, St. John's University's College of Business Administration and St. John's Law School, as well as a strong work ethic. With it in hand, I started my quest to become an assistant district attorney. However, I lacked a critical requirement for those jobs. I lacked a rabbi. No, not a rabbi in the religious sense of the word, but a rabbi who presided at services in the world of politics. In Queens County, you and your rabbi had to be a Democrat. Across the county lines in Nassau and Suffolk, the predominant secular religion was Republican. Great.

Mom and Dad did not have any political connections. To make things worse, I registered as a Conservative, a choice disliked by Democrats and Republicans alike, in the election that saw James L. Buckley become New York's United States Senator in 1970.

Notwithstanding that decision, I almost got a job in Westchester County. I was told I passed the initial interview with flying colors, and a second interview was scheduled with the chief of the trial bureau, who then took me to see the chief assistant. The next day, I got a call to schedule a meeting with the district attorney himself. I was assured by the chief that this was merely a formality. However, no one told that to the DA and no one bothered to mention to him that I was of Italian descent, although you would think that my last name alone would have been a sufficient clue.

After a cordial meeting with the DA, including a discussion of where my family came from in Italy, we discussed my future. Unfortunately, my future did not include *a position with the Westchester District Attorney's Office. "Gregg," he said, "you're more than qualified, but I have to be honest with you. I have too many Italians on my staff, and that doesn't look good." So said the district attorney who was himself of Italian origin.*

My hoped-for career as a prosecutor came to an abrupt end. Given my desire to practice criminal law, the only choice I had was to go over to the dark side and work for the defense.

I felt that Nassau County would be a good place to practice. It was not as hectic as Queens or Brooklyn but not as slow-paced as Suffolk. In short, it was a Goldilocks spot—just the right place to learn how to become a criminal defense attorney.

My first and only interview at Legal Aid lasted over three hours, and I was interviewed by at least four senior members of that office. The last lawyer to interview me that day was Peter Lazarus (who you'll meet in the next chapter). Peter offered me the job on the spot, and my legal career began.

Legal Aid was staffed by an eclectic group of attorneys, some just out of law school, some with years of experience and others practicing law as a second career. Schools like Harvard, Chicago Law and NYU were represented. I was told at the start of my job that the chips would be against us as we would be fighting daily with the experience and resources of the Nassau County District Attorney's Office. The only hope of winning was to out lawyer, out work and outsmart the prosecution. Sometimes it worked.

I met with Benny while he was still in jail, and I met with Nina at the scene of the crime. I quickly understood that Benny was a law-abiding individual, a hard-working father, and generally a good guy... as long as he took his medication. Much as a diabetic needs insulin, Benny needed to take his medication daily to lead a normal life. The problem was, Benny did not want to take his medication. When he stopped taking the medication, Benny was back in the Japanese prisoner-of-war camp of his delusions.

In our discussions, Benny promised both Nina and me that if he were released from jail, he would take the new medication ordered by the psychiatrist. With the help of family and friends, Nina was able to come up with $5,000 in cash for bail. The kindly county court judge assigned to Benny's case, the Honorable Vincent Tally, patiently listened to my bail application and, upon extracting from Benny the promise he would continue to take his lithium, set the bail as I requested.

The Nassau County District Attorney's Office, however, was not so magnanimous when we tried to dispose of the case prior to trial. While their plea offer to reduce the charge of criminal possession of a weapon from a felony to a misdemeanor was reasonable under the circumstances, the ADA insisted the court impose a one-year jail sentence as a condition of accepting the plea. While the court seemed amenable to my request for a sentence of probation, the DA's office held firm, in large part because Benny had threatened to kill two police officers.

"Take the one year in jail or go to trial" was the DA's position in a nutshell.

While fighting the DA's office, I was also fighting Benny. He refused to plead guilty to *anything*.

His position was clear: "I was in my own home—my castle—and I did not hurt anyone."

Getting through to Benny was as difficult as getting through to the DA's office. Neither would budge an inch, so the case that should *never* have been tried had to be.

From the defense perspective, a trial on these facts was destined to result in a quick verdict of guilty. However, there was one strategy we could use to give us a shot at winning. When I approached Benny with the trial strategy of arguing temporary insanity, he would not hear of it. He was not insane, not even temporarily. He kept insisting, over and over again (you guessed it), "I was in my own house, and no one got hurt anyway." And that was it. Clearly, this was going to be a one-sided trial.

The trial lasted three days. The People's case consisted of testimony from Patrolman Gugliamenti, Detective Sergeant Kite, several police officers who were on the scene that day and an officer from the department's ballistics unit. He testified that the rifle in Benny's possession was a Savage Model 110 .308-caliber deer rifle loaded with a three-shot magazine, and when he examined the rifle, he found an additional round in the chamber. Most importantly, the officer testified that the rifle was operational and capable of discharging a bullet.

The defense consisted of cross-examining the People's witnesses to show that Benny lacked the criminal intent to commit the charged crimes. Definitely a stretch, but it was all that we had.

The People's case concluded at about eleven on a Friday morning. I rested Benny's case without calling a single witness. The trial was over except for the summations by both sides and the court's charge to the jury on the law applicable to the case. The ADA and I both looked forward to having the weekend to draft our requests to the court for specific language to use in its jury charge and to put the final touches on our summations, but that soon would change.

After eleven years on the county court bench and many years before that in the district court, Judge Tally knew a slam-dunk case when he saw it. "Gentlemen," he said after he retired the jury for lunch, "be back here at one-thirty with your requests to charge and be ready to sum up at two o'clock."

The sly old judge probably figured he could have the charge to the jury completed by three-thirty with verdict shortly thereafter and still be home in time for Friday night cocktails. This tactic would also open up the judge's calendar for Monday morning so he would be able to catch up on his other cases, which had to be postponed due to our trial.

The summations and jury charge were, in fact, completed by four o'clock. As the jurors filed out of the courtroom to deliberate, the traditional bets were being placed. Much like those casting lots for the Savior's cloak, the court officers generally made bets on how long it would take for the jury to bring in a verdict. The game was simple: kick in a dollar and pick a time the jury would return its verdict. To increase the size of the pot, the ADA, defense counsel and any police officers in the courtroom were permitted entry into the pool.

In Benny's case, a quick guilty verdict was anticipated. One officer even bet it would take "as long as it takes for all twelve jurors to take a piss and vote—twenty minutes." His colleagues were of a like mind, and the last bet was for five-thirty. It was mine.

Five-thirty came and went. So did six-thirty. "Maybe the jurors will feel better after dinner," a court officer said as he went on the sandwich run.

Seven-thirty and eight-thirty also dragged by, and all that could be heard in the cavernous rotunda outside the courtroom was the sound of shoes pacing on the polished marble floors.

The courtroom we were in was one of four on the first floor of the county courthouse in Mineola. It was large and could hold upwards of a hundred people in the spectator section. The spectators' area was separated from the well, where the lawyers and defendants sat by a three-foot-high railing wall with swinging gates at each end. Two six-foot-long tables, one for the defense and one for the prosecution, were located in the well, ten feet apart on either side of center. To the right of the prosecutors table was the jury box with chairs for the twelve jurors and two alternate jurors who would serve in the event that one or two of the twelve became incapacitated during the trial or deliberations. Another twelve or so feet in front of the counsel tables stood the judge's bench. It was raised three feet above the floor, along with the witness stand and an area for the clerk of the court, who was in charge of calling cases, swearing in witnesses and recording the proceedings in the court's files.

All of the wood in the room was a dark mahogany color. The bronze *In God We Trust* seal hung above the judge's high-backed black chair. Six ten-foot windows, three on each side of the room, allowed light to filter in.

But on this night, no light shone in, and even the six chandeliers that hung from the vaulted ceiling provided only a cream-colored glow. To me, the courtroom appeared as an empty cave, cold and dark, occupied by only the court officers, the ADA, Detective Kite and the three of us—Benny, Nina and me. The rest of the humans occupying the cave were hidden behind closed doors in the judge's chambers or the jury room, guarded by two additional court officers.

The rotunda also had a scary feeling at night. Gone was the hectic activity of lawyers running in and out of the courtrooms and the milling about of clients and family members. It was dark, cold and sterile, with only a few night lights turned on. The space could have been used by Steven Spielberg for *Raiders of the Lost Ark*; all that was missing were the spiders and snakes.

Groups of court officers, along with the ADA and Detective Kite, would strike up small discussions to kill the monotony of waiting. At times, I, Nina and even Benny, were invited into the various conversations, such as it is with boredom. I was taken by the fact that Kite held no animosity towards Benny and Benny none for Kite. The detective was tough, no doubt about it, but he was also a guy with a heart. Most of his cases involved criminals he called "mutts and dirt bags" who needed to be taken out of circulation. Kite never thought that way about Benny, and he told me so in several conversations that we had that night, when we were not discussing the New York Mets' Tom Seaver and Tug McGraw.

The eerie quiet of the courthouse, akin to the quiet of the medical examiner's office, was shattered at about 11:30 p.m. (yes, we were still there), when we heard the loud echo of footsteps approaching the courtroom. The door swung open and Harold J. Funderburk, the chief clerk of the county court appeared. Harold and his wife had been heading to their Garden City home after a party when he saw the courthouse lights were still blazing. True to his reputation of being a stickler for details, as well as a class A ballbuster, Harold just had to investigate what was going on "in MY courthouse."

As soon as his cranky visage appeared at the courtroom door, every court officer, of whom there were five, sprang into action, the likes of which none of us had seen in the three days of trial. Everyone was eager to give their views on the case to the chief. This was completely useless, as the chief knew everything. Looking to show once again that he was indeed the chief—and a brilliant chief at that—he told a court officer to bring him the rifle.

"It's in with the jury, sir," the senior court officer said.

"Well then, how about the bullets?"

A quick response came. "All the exhibits are in with the jury, Chief."

I looked at Kite. The ADA looked at Kite. Kite looked up at heaven.

So there we were: it was almost midnight in a place that now resembled a morgue, as opposed to a courthouse, and twelve people, with probably no experience in dealing with a firearm, were locked in a fifteen-by-ten-foot room with an operable .308 deer rifle and live ammunition. The chief went—appropriately, I believe—berserk.

"How could you have let this happen?" he bellowed at the court personnel.

Immediately, the judge was summoned from his office and was told by the chief that while the jurors could have all the trial exhibits during their deliberations, he strongly suggested that the rifle and bullets be kept separate and only one of the exhibits be allowed in the jury room at the same time, "before someone gets killed."

The judge ordered the senior court officer to knock immediately on the door of the jury's deliberation room and remove the bullets. Thankfully, after close to eight hours of deliberation, not one of the jurors wanted to see if the rifle really worked.

Finally, at 1:40 a.m., the jury reached the expected verdict of guilty on both counts. While the ADA sought to remand Benny to jail pending sentence, the exhausted but still sympathetic judge continued the posted $5,000 bail and ordered that Benny go to the county probation department for the preparation of the obligatory presentence report and then return to court in eight weeks for sentencing.

As Benny, Nina and I left the courthouse and entered the deserted parking lot facing the Nassau County Supreme Court, I shook Benny's hand, looked him in the eye and said, "Behave yourself."

For the next five weeks, I hardly gave Benny Bearachi a thought. I had two and a half file drawers filled with cases of clients who needed representation. I was in court each morning and spent the afternoons interviewing clients both in and out of the county jail, meeting with our investigators who were uncovering facts to be used at upcoming trials and writing motions. Time was tight.

One afternoon, I needed to work on a brief in support of my motion to suppress a revolver the police had seized in what I contended was an illegal search. The motion was due in two days time, and I had been so busy the previous two weeks, I had not even started the legal research. I called my wife, Charleen, to tell her I would not be home for dinner and not for hours after that.

My desk was cluttered with law books as I tried to find a New York Court of Appeals or a Federal Second Circuit case to support my novel theory. I was in for a long night.

Then, the phone rang. We had an unwritten rule at Legal Aid: never answer the phone after 5:00 p.m.

In those days, caller ID did not exist, so when my phone rang at around five forty-five, I let it do so. Ten minutes later, the phone rang again, only this time for much longer. The phone that was ringing was my line, not the general office number. I let it ring again, trying to concentrate on my legal research. A few minutes later, the phone rang for a third time, and curiosity got the best of me. I picked it up.

"Gregg, it's Nina. Benny has gone berserk again."

From the tone of her voice, I could feel her panic. I asked if she and the kids were OK and she assured me they were at her neighbor's house.

Then Nina continued, "Benny stopped taking his meds, and while we were all eating dinner, he snapped again. He jumped out of his seat and flung his plate of lasagna against the kitchen wall. Then he started smashing the dinner plates. That's when I ran out with the kids. You've got to come and help."

I asked Nina if there were any weapons in the house, and she said that there were none, aside from the usual kitchen knives.

When I suggested Nina call the police, she said "You remember the last time I did that. You are the only one Benny trusts."

How could I turn her down? I told Nina to remain at her friend's house and that I would be over as soon as I could get there. I called Charleen to let her know what was happening and that I would be home even later than originally planned. When she asked what I was going to do, I recall saying that I wasn't sure.

She cautioned, "Don't do anything stupid."

As I gathered my coat to go to Benny's house, Charleen's word "stupid" rang in my ears. What in God's name was I going to do? I was five foot eleven and weighed one hundred and sixty pounds. I was not going to be able to confront Benny, who was several inches taller than me and outweighed me by at least ninety pounds. Although Benny was far from muscular, he was a bear of a man. There was no way I would be able to control him alone. The more I thought about it, the more I thought it was insanity to go there alone. But who could help?

After reflecting for a few moments, I knew there was only one person I could call for help. I reached into my wallet to get a business card that I was given that long night we spent pacing the rotunda floor in the courthouse. Even though our interactions were brief, I felt he was a man of his word and could be trusted. I had to go on my instincts. A trial attorney develops a sixth sense about people. It's an essential skill for picking a jury, the ability to analyze a person as friend or foe in the space of minutes. I picked up the phone.

Operator: Crime Prevention Unit.

Me: Detective Sergeant Kite, please.

Operator: He is out in the field. Can I help you?

Me: No, it's an emergency. Can you please try to reach him and ask him to call me back?

After leaving my office number with CPU, I cleared my desk of all those law books and waited for my phone to ring. I had all sorts of doubts in my mind about whether my call would be returned but had to hope.

About ten minutes later, my phone rang again. It was Kite. After I repeated the story to the detective, I told him I was going to Benny's house. Before I could ask for his help, Kite told me to meet him and two members of his team around the block from Benny's house in twenty minutes. He also asked if I was still driving the Robin's Egg. Kite recalled the story I told him the night we were waiting for the jury to reach their verdict, the story about my 1968 VW Beetle. It was originally dark blue. There were so many scratches on it that I decided to have it re-painted with an Earl Scheib $99 paint special. I told the manager of the paint shop that I wanted the bug painted a lighter shade of blue. When I picked up the car, it was painted robin's egg blue. I originally wanted to have the car repainted, but the color grew on me.

"You got it, Sarge. See you there," I said, grateful and relieved.

Fifteen minutes later, I pulled the Egg into a parking space around the corner from Benny's house.

A beat-up old Ford pulled behind me, and two scruffy looking guys in their late twenties approached my car. "You the Legal Aid guy?" they asked, flashing their gold detective shields.

"Yeah, I'm glad you guys decided to come out and help."

"It was Sarge's idea," came a very cold and annoyed response.

We stood by their vehicle waiting for Kite, and he did not disappoint. As soon as his Ford Crown Vic arrived, we all huddled around it to devise our strategy. I persuaded him to let me go in the house and speak to Benny to find out what was going on. Kite then asked where my briefcase was, and I told him it was in the Egg. I was then directed to get it and follow his rules "very carefully and exactly."

This was our game plan. I would have fifteen minutes to go in, speak to Benny and assess the situation. After fifteen minutes, I would tell Benny I had to get something from my car and leave the house. I was to stay in the living room with the large picture window at my back. The police would be watching through that window, and if I felt threatened by Benny and needed help, the signal would be my throwing the briefcase against the front window. If that eventuality occurred, I was directed, in terms that no one could misunderstand, to hit the floor and let Kite and the boys take it from there.

As I got back in my car, Kite put his hand on my shoulder, looked me straight in the eye and said, "Remember, there is only one Wacky Wilson. Don't do anything stupid." I guess both my wife and Kite had the same opinion of me.

Admittedly, I did not know what to expect nor what I could do to diffuse the situation. Things were happening so fast that I did not have the chance to be scared, that is, until I approached the front door at 47 Padre Road. It was ajar.

I opened it about a foot and said, "Benny, it's Gregg. Can I come in?"

His voice was surprisingly calm. "Come on in; it's cold out there tonight."

I started to push the door open, and as I did, I heard a clinking sound and met some resistance. As soon as I had the door open enough to get myself and the briefcase through, I understood the reason for the clinking. The floor was covered with smashed pottery and dishware. The pile must have been at least a half-inch thick in the foyer. It looked like every vase, plant pot and anything else ceramic in the house was busted and strewn on the floor.

Disregarding Kite's instructions, I walked about ten feet, over the shattered pottery toward the kitchen, where Benny was sitting at the table as if nothing had happened.

As I was doing so, a quick glance out of the picture window was comforting. I saw the Crown Vic parked across the street with its lights out. In the kitchen, the remnants of what once had been the family's dishware, along with silverware and various pots and pans, littered the floor. Smashed glass covered the rest of the destruction like a snowfall.

The exploded remains of a pan of homemade lasagna joined Benny's dinner plate and dripped down one wall. The red of the tomato sauce, the browned mozzarella, the white of the ricotta and the tan noodles looked like a strangely out of place Jackson Pollack creation. While I have had many plates of lasagna, this vision of my favorite pasta dish was in a strange way artistically pleasing—but for the rage one must have felt to create it.

Mindful that I was now out of CPU's sight, I asked Benny to join me in the living room, which for some reason was untouched by the rampage. I only had about half of my allotted fifteen minutes left. I asked Benny what was going on. It was after his initial response that I became scared. Benny, who acknowledged he stopped taking his lithium "a few days ago," proceeded to tell me his vision of things:

"Nina, the judge and you are conspiring against me. What the three of you have done is to recreate both Nassau County and my home and place it in Wisconsin. But you guys made a big mistake. When I went to the grocery store yesterday, I saw the Swiss cheese in the dairy case and the label said it was made in Wisconsin. So we have to be in Wisconsin. If we were really in Nassau, we would have Swiss cheese from New York."

Not even Aristotle could quibble with Benny's logic. And, of course, there was no talking Benny out of his perception. Therefore, I didn't even try. Up until that comment, I believed that I was in control of the situation. Now I wasn't too sure, and the anger in his voice only magnified my concern. If he thought I was part of the conspiracy, I could be in danger. I suggested that Benny and I take

31

a ride two miles up the road to Meadowbrook Hospital so he could discuss the situation with the doctors there. Surprisingly, Benny did not put up any resistance to that suggestion.

The only condition he demanded was that he be able to interview the doctor who would be speaking to him to determine "if the doctor came from Wisconsin." Of course, I readily agreed.

As the fifteen-minute time limit was drawing to a close, I told Benny I would get my car and pick him up in his driveway. I walked again over the shards of dishware, left the house and walked around the corner to the prearranged meeting spot. Kite was already there. Soon, the two CPU cops, who were previously stationed on either side of Benny's front door while I was inside, appeared. The fact that one of the officers was carrying a shotgun only seemed to heighten the sense of danger.

I told Kite that Benny had agreed to go to the hospital with me. The game plan Kite then concocted was simple and quick. He would call the Meadowbrook Hospital emergency room. The Nassau County Police Department had an officer stationed there 24/7. This officer was directed to have a psychiatrist ready to see Benny as soon as we pulled up. Kite did not want to have a potentially dangerous and deranged man who had just trashed his own home sitting in an overcrowded ER waiting room. It was my hope that the psychiatrist would determine Benny was a danger to himself or others and have him involuntarily committed to the psych ward. Then, after a few days back on lithium, I hoped Benny would be fine and be released to go home.

Getting Benny to Meadowbrook was our next hurdle. Kite wanted an ambulance to take him because he was concerned that the mentally unstable Benny sitting next to me in a VW Bug was too dangerous. He could decide to grab the wheel and crash the car. I told Kite that the arrival of an ambulance would frighten Benny and he could repeat the scene that Kite had already lived through once. Reluctantly, Kite agreed on the condition that I follow a route to the hospital using back streets. Finally, I pulled the VW into Benny's driveway. Benny was already on his stoop and laughing at the Egg. Laughter, I thought, was a good sign. When Benny got into the car wearing his winter overcoat, the seatbelt would not fit him. We sat shoulder to shoulder. I put the four-speed stick into reverse, and we started down the driveway toward the hospital.

Benny sat calmly as we proceeded down the street—first gear, second gear and finally third gear, which was as fast as Kite wanted me to drive. As I stopped at the first stop sign, I saw Kite's blue Crown Vic behind me. I went straight ahead and the Crown Vic made a right turn as a green Ford I had just passed left the curb and was now on my tail. As I made the next right turn, the Ford proceeded straight ahead, and the Crown Vic pulled in behind me. Just like in the old movies, when one tail broke off, the other tail began. I pulled the Egg directly in front of the ER, ignoring the Do Not Park sign.

After I helped Benny out of the car, a uniformed police officer stepped up and directed us to a room in the ER. We walked right by a number of people who'd waited a long time to be seen. There was some muttering behind us. This room was not one of the typical curtained bays found in most ERs. It was a room with walls, about nine feet by eight feet, with a wide doorway that a stretcher could be easily pushed through. Only a few uneasy minutes passed before the psychiatrist on call appeared.

When I started to explain why we were there, this young doctor, a second-year resident, shut me up quickly, snapping, "I know why you're here. Please leave so I can speak to my patient."

I walked out to the police desk. Kite was there. I shook his hand and thanked him for his help and said I would stay just in case I was needed by the rather brusque and annoyed psychiatrist. Kite left and I went back into the waiting room and found a chair. Less than thirty minutes later, Dr. Greenstein, so proclaimed by a shiny white Meadowbrook Hospital name tag, appeared and told me in a clipped English accent: "You can take Mr. Bearachi home."

I was shocked.

I reminded the good doctor that this guy just terrorized his family, destroyed his kitchen and asked, "You think he can go home?"

Dr. Greenstein shot me the "I am the doctor" look and said, "I am discharging him from the ER. What you do with him is your business. He can wait in the exam room while you get your car."

My business indeed! Now what? I was not going to take Benny home, nor could I just abandon him in the crowded ER. I paid another visit to the police liaison desk. "Can you locate Wilson Kite for me?" In minutes, Kite was on the police radio, and as I relayed my discussion with Dr. Greenstein, Kite became more and more pissed.

Less than ten minutes later, the door to the ER flung opened and Kite roared through it like a heat-seeking missile just fired from a fighter jet. He did not stop to speak either to me or the liaison officer. He went directly to the chief resident's office. Shortly thereafter, Dr. Greenstein was paged by the chief resident to his office and came face-to-face with Kite. Words like "murder," "on your conscience" and "potential suicide" flew out of his mouth and were audible in the waiting room. Whether Dr. Greenstein was convinced or just plain scared of Kite, his decision to discharge Benny was quickly reversed. Dr. Greenstein's next chart note stated that Benny was a danger to himself and possibly others and had to be held for psychiatric evaluation.

Greenstein now needed me. He knew that Benny and I had a relationship, and he hoped Benny would listen to me. Greenstein asked me to persuade Benny to go with the orderlies up to the psych floor—without having a brawl ensue. Two men dressed in white coats and who were even larger than Benny waited outside the exam room. They stood like two icebergs guarding the room. When I entered the room with Dr. Greenstein, the two men followed, blocking any possible escape by Benny. One iceberg held a straitjacket behind his back out of Benny's sight.

Benny was calm as I told him he had to stay the night. He sat on the exam table looking at Dr. Greenstein and me but avoided looking at the two men guarding the door. He asked Greenstein what city in Wisconsin we were in, but when the doctor failed to respond, Benny let it go. After a few seconds that seemed like minutes, Benny asked for a cigarette. Smoking was not allowed in the Meadowbrook Hospital emergency room, but the iceberg on the left walked forward and offered Benny an unfiltered cigarette. Benny sat passively on the exam table, puffing on the butt. Greenstein shot me a knowing look, as if to say that with all these big bodies in such a small room, there would be little space for him and me to take cover if violence erupted. Indeed, it could have gotten very messy. Then, halfway finished with the cigarette, Benny stood. Was this the start of Benny's escape from the ER? The tension level in the room spiked in a millisecond. Surprisingly, Benny looked around the room, threw the still burning cigarette on the floor and said in a quiet tone, "Let's go."

Benny walked peacefully to the elevator with the orderlies and Dr. Greenstein without being put in a straitjacket and disappeared into the elevator. It was now well past midnight, and even though it was the middle of March, my light blue shirt was soaking wet. When I went out to find Kite and offer to buy him a drink, much like the Lone Ranger, he was nowhere to be found.

<hr/>

I never saw Detective Sergeant Wilson Kite after that, but he is someone I shall never forget. His toughness tempered with understanding and compassion was special. I hope there is a little of Wacky Wilson in all law enforcement officers as they conduct their duty of protecting all citizens.

Benny was discharged from the hospital after three days of being back on lithium. The probation department's pre-sentence report recommended that Benny be placed on probation with psychiatric conditions. Accordingly, Judge Tally, over objection by the DA's office, followed the recommendation and sentenced Benny to five years on probation.

During my remaining two years at Legal Aid, I never heard from either Benny or Nina, nor did I hear that Benny violated probation. They were nice people struggling to cope with Benny's mental illness and raise their two children. I hope they made it and are happy together.

But I think of them every time I eat a plate of lasagna.

⌒ 2 ⌒

September 1971

A Time *Not* to Die

None of the holiday travelers heading east on the Long Island Expressway bothered to take a second look at the nondescript gray 1966 Corvair traveling in the right lane slightly below the posted speed limit. Had they done so, they would have seen that the passenger in the front seat sat at an odd angle, looking back at the two men in the rear. The Corvair took exit 49 to Bagatelle Road. Three hundred yards down the road, the car stopped next to a patch of woods to unload its human cargo from the back seat.

"Time to get out, gents," the man in the front passenger seat said. He held a shiny .22-caliber revolver just inches from their faces.

The younger backseat passenger, Rick Cooper, slowly opened the door and got out, followed by the middle-aged Fabrizo (Fabby) DiFrono.

An hour before, nineteen-year-old Rick Cooper was stocking the shelves in the paper aisle at the Waldbaum's supermarket in Plainview. It was Saturday night, and he looked forward to having the next two days off for the

Labor Day weekend. Just five minutes left, he thought, as he glanced at his watch. While he continued to open cases of paper towels with his razor box cutter and then mark each individual roll with its price from his rotary stamp, his mind wandered. He planned to meet his friends after work tonight and go to Monday's barbecue with his date, the cute seventeen-year-old red-haired cashier. He was shocked back to reality when someone on the PA system ordered, "Rick Cooper, report to the manager's office."

The store manager, Fabby DiFrono, was in a joyous mood. Fabby had been with Waldbaum's for more than ten years and, before that, had managed a store for a competing chain. He could not recall a busier holiday weekend in all those years. The cashiers worked nonstop and Fabby expected record receipts. It seemed like everyone in Plainview was trying to get in one more weekend of summer before the cold Long Island winter set in with its usual snowfalls. The same was true for Fabby. He planned to take his wife and two children out to Montauk early Sunday morning and spend the next two days enjoying the sun and the ocean at Gurney's Inn. All that was left to do was to prepare the daily cash bank deposit and go home.

With the last customer checked out, the deposit ritual began. The head cashier closed out each of the nine registers and brought the money to the manager's office. There, she would count the cash and prepare the deposit ticket. Fabby would then count it again, and if the count matched, he would initial the deposit ticket and place the cash in the deposit pouch provided by the bank, which was located a mere eight doors down the strip mall. The final step in the deposit dance, choreographed by the store's insurance carrier, required two people to witness the pouch being dropped into the bank's night depository chute. Fabby or the assistant store manager, Shawn Pagano, usually performed that task with one of the stock boys. That night, Fabby and Rick Cooper would take the deposit to the bank.

"We'll be right back, then we'll lock up and get the hell out of here," Fabby told Erica Christina, the head cashier, as the two men headed out the front door.

Outside the store, the parking lot was nearly empty. Customers and shop owners had fled the strip mall for more enjoyable pursuits. Nevertheless, a gray Corvair cruised slowly up and down the parking lot aisles. Sometimes, the Corvair would back in and stop in a parking stall directly in front of the bank. Then it would pull out again and make another loop. The odd behavior of the car and its occupants caught the eye of Betty Budzick, the owner of Betty's Beauty Boutique, located halfway between the supermarket and the bank. At about 8:45 p.m., Betty had started to redecorate her front window for the fall season.

When the car's occupants got out to wander up and down the sidewalks in front of the stores, she thought they made a strange looking pair. The driver looked to be about fifty years old, was tall and had distinctive rodent-like facial features. The much younger and shorter of the two looked like the greaser Bernardo in *West Side Story* with his black leather jacket and his long black hair combed back high on his head and held in place with a substance resembling petroleum jelly. Betty even observed the younger fellow peering into her boutique's front glass window to ogle her twenty-one-year-old stylist, who was finishing up their last customer. Even though the two guys weren't doing anything wrong, their appearances gave Betty the creeps. At about 9:15 p.m., Betty closed the shop and walked to her car. For some reason she couldn't explain, even to herself, Betty took a pen out of her coiffed hair and jotted down the Corvair's license plate number, SKJ-7419, on the brown bag that contained her groceries from Waldbaum's.

As Fabby and Rick walked to the bank with the drop pouch that contained $13,725, mostly in fives, tens, some twenties and even a few fifties, the two Yankees fans commiserated about their team's lousy season. They barely noticed the young man in a black leather jacket looking into the window of the gift shop they had just passed. As they approached the bank, they were unaware that the same man followed them.

At the night depository box, Fabby reached for the handle to pull down the chute. As soon as he did, he felt a cold metal object directly under his right ear and heard the words, "Give me the money."

Although he was scared, Fabby remembered his corporate training when it came to robberies: do nothing to cause injury to any customer or employee. He held the bank pouch over his head, and it was quickly snatched by the robber. Rick just stood there frozen. "How could this be happening?" he kept thinking to himself.

With all the action going on at the bank drop, neither Rick nor Fabby noticed that the Corvair had pulled up to the curb and the back door closest to the sidewalk had flung open.

"Get in the car. Now," the greaser with the gun ordered.

This command had to be repeated twice before the stunned victims could react. Immediately upon entering the car, the captives were ordered to place their hands behind their backs. They did as they were told. Both men instinctively knew that lunging for the gun would result in either one or both of them being shot or killed. Rick felt the razor box cutter in his back pocket. It was a weapon, but he remembered an old saying about not bringing a knife to a gunfight.

Rick and Fabby independently decided to wait for a better chance to resist their captors. Besides, Fabby had some praying to do.

The car took off heading east down Old Country Road. Neither the driver with the rodent-like features nor the greaser with the gun made any effort to hide their faces. The Corvair was a compact car, and all the way to Bagatelle Road, the gunman in the passenger seat sat sideways, looking both Rick and Fabby in the eye, his finger on the trigger of the revolver inches away from their faces.

When Fabby and Rickey failed to get back to the store in five minutes, Erica became anxious. She wanted to get home. After ten minutes, she left the store and looked up the block towards the bank and saw no sign of either man. She called Fabby's name several times, and when no response was forthcoming, she became frightened. She returned to the store, locked the door, picked up the phone and called the police.

"Second Precinct, Officer Bateman," a voice said.

"This is Erica Christina, the head cashier at the Plainview Waldbaum's, and I think we have been robbed."

———

When Fabby and Rick got the gunman's order to get out of the car, Fabby's body went numb. He could not feel his hands or feet. His brain shut down because he felt sure he was going to die. If this were just about the money, he and Rick would have been left at the bank. They had spent fifteen minutes face-to-face with both perpetrators, and that meant he and Rick could give their descriptions to the police. The greaser looked like a mean SOB, and Fabby was astute enough to know his fate. Luckily for Rick, he was unable to see the writing on the wall.

As they got out of the car, Fabby and Rick found themselves on a rarely used service road of the Long Island Expressway. The expressway lay a hundred yards behind them and a small forest of pine trees stood before them.

"Just walk down the hill toward those pines," the gunman ordered.

As they did, the greaser followed them about twenty feet behind. Fabby started to pick up the pace, hoping the woods would give them some protection from the lunatic with the gun. Rick and Fabby approached a dirt mound. Fabby took a path around the mound, while Rick walked straight up the two-foot hill. As he reached the summit, Rick heard a loud bang. He turned to his left and saw Fabby fall to the ground like a sack of potatoes. Now Rick faced the gunman. The greaser fired a second round from his Saturday night special. The bullet found its mark into Rick's midsection, and he fell. He was stunned, unable to think beyond a recognition that he was alive. Instinct told him to lie still. He heard heavy footsteps receding and then fading away.

Although Rick heard the car speed off, he was still in shock from what occurred. He remained on the ground. He could hear Fabby's moaning, but he was too scared to move until he was sure the crazed gunman was gone. When he felt certain the gunman wasn't coming back, Rick slowly got to his feet. Even though he had a sharp pain in his gut—like a hard punch to the stomach—he was surprised that he was not bleeding. But Fabby was.

The gunshot wound in Fabby's back turned his white Waldbaum's shirt crimson. Rick pulled off his belt. It was made of leather and had a big heavy metal buckle, like most of the teenagers he knew wore. He used it as a tourniquet around Fabby's midsection to try and stop the blood.

That would help, but not for long. Fabby was bleeding to death.

Rick ran back up the hill towards the service road. About fifty yards to the left of the service road, cars were whizzing by on the expressway, but Rick's path to them was blocked by a six-foot-high cyclone fence. As he thought about scaling the fence, he saw headlights coming down the service road. Rick ran into the middle of the road and waived his arms frantically. The driver had no choice but to stop or run Rick over.

"I need help," Ricky said. "My boss has been shot."

The driver left his car on the shoulder of the road and followed Rick. Within minutes, Rick and the driver carried Fabby up the hill and got him into the car's back

44

seat. Rick kept pressure on the wound as the driver sped down the service road, made the first possible left turn and headed for Route 110. Once there, he made another left and sped to Brunswick Hospital in Amityville.

—

The neoclassical old courthouse was situated on the corner of Old County Road and Franklin Avenue in Mineola. Its cornerstone was laid by Governor Teddy Roosevelt in 1900 and its magnificent dome dominated the surrounding skyline. As Nassau County grew from a farming community to a suburb, a new courthouse was needed and was built a few blocks farther east in the late 1930s. The old courthouse was then used for various county offices. When space became tight in police headquarters two blocks to the south, the old courthouse received some new tenants: the department's homicide, robbery and arson squads, as well as the crime prevention unit.

On this night, the robbery squad was manned by two of its most seasoned detectives, Lenny Scuderi and Hank Kosinski. Lenny and Hank had been partners for over six years and had investigated and, more importantly, solved many cases together. Lenny was short and muscular. He was always attired in a well-pressed dark suit and white shirt accented by a tie that matched his pocket square. His black hair was neatly combed back and held in place with hairspray. Hank was thinner, taller and cared less about his appearance. A reference to Laurel and Hardy fit the duo, but none of the other guys on the squad had the guts to make the comment within hearing range. It was about 10:00 p.m. when the squad's phone rang. Hank took the squeal. He jotted down the info on a scrap of yellow paper and then shouted to Lenny, who was filing case reports.

"The Waldbaum's in Plainview just got hit. Two employees missing; might be a kidnapping as well."

Usually, when Lenny and Hank got a call, there was no sense rushing. The robbery had already occurred, and uniformed cops from the local precinct were securing the scene. But this one was different—a possible kidnapping. Rarely did this occur, but when it did, the outcome for the victims usually resulted in a one-way van ride in a black body bag to the county's medical examiner's office.

The detectives retrieved service revolvers from their desk drawers and headed for their unmarked Crown Victoria, as they had countless times before. This time, they ran.

As they approached their exit on the expressway, police dispatch radioed: "The ER at Brunswick Hospital just reported two male patients—gunshot wounds—claimed to be robbery victims from Waldbaum's—one in surgery—they matched the description of the two missing employees."

Hank took a hard right and headed for the Southern State Parkway and then east to Amityville.

The Brunswick Hospital emergency room was always a busy place. It was located in a poorer section of Suffolk County just over the Nassau border, and it served as a doctor's office for many of the area's residents. The Brunswick ER doctors were no strangers to knife and gunshot wounds, as this part of Suffolk had more than its share of each.

When Lenny and Hank entered the ER, a nurse

directed them to Dr. Michael Bender, the attending physician in charge. They showed their detective shields to Dr. Bender. He motioned them into an empty bay at the rear of the ER.

There, Dr. Bender presented the cases: "One male, forty-five years old, named Fabrizo DiFrono, but he goes by Fabby, is the manager at the Plainview Waldbaum's, according to an ID in his wallet. He was brought in via automobile in an unconscious state, gunshot wound to the lower right quadrant of his back. We don't know if the bullet hit his spinal cord or did much damage to his kidneys or liver. He has lost a lot of blood, and we have given him three units already. He is in surgery now. We won't know how he will do until surgery is completed. My guess is he will make it, but he could be paralyzed. I just don't know."

"How about the second victim?" Lenny asked. "What kind of shape is he in?"

The expression on Dr. Bender's face changed quickly and dramatically. While he had just given the detectives the DiFrono medical pass-down in a quick, concise, professional manner, his face now showed confusion.

"He complains of a pain in his gut, but he is not shot, stabbed, beaten or anything. His name is Rick Cooper, age nineteen, works as a stock boy at Waldbaum's. He is a student at Hofstra University studying criminology."

After hearing Bender's report, the detectives' first thoughts led them to the same conclusion: The kid was in on a robbery that went sour and a guy got shot.

The two officers decided that Hank, who looked the friendlier of the two, would take the first crack at interviewing Rick. Lenny would follow up with the police units on the scene and direct that all the shopkeepers in the strip mall be interviewed to see if anyone noted anything suspicious. He wanted whatever information Waldbaum's had on Rick, including a list of his friends. Lenny also learned Mrs. DiFrono was on her way to the hospital. He would have to hold her hand when she got there.

"I hate this part of the job," Lenny thought. Even though his physical appearance resembled Friar Tuck with a lot of hair, he was never able to generate the consoling persona he needed at times like this. Tonight would be no different, with a crying wife begging him to promise Fabby wouldn't die. Lenny would tell her that her husband would make it, then pray that the prediction came true. He wanted that for the family, and he also wanted it for the benefit of his case.

The interview technique Lenny and Hank used would be the standard good cop/bad cop drill they had modified in their years of experience working as a team. Many times, it was successful, and the team of Scuderi and Kosinski got more than their share of perps to confess their sins. The charming Hank would get Rick's story, and then, Lenny would hammer the suspect with any inconsistencies with the facts coming in from the crime scene.

"Physical evidence does not lie," Lenny had roared at many a suspect.

But that was round two. Hank had to get round one under his belt first. They decided to interrogate Rick at the hospital instead of transporting him to the robbery squad. While being in a police station interrogation room was stressful, they thought that holding the questioning at the hospital, where Fabby's life was in the balance and where the cries of his wife and two young kids could be heard down the hall, would put Rick under more psychological pressure.

As he collected his thoughts for the interrogation, Hank reviewed the facts as he knew them, and several questions crossed his mind. Was Rick in on the robbery? If so, why did Rick try to save Fabby's life? If he was in on the robbery, his accomplices would not have let him do that. Or did Rick get a conscience after Fabby was shot and he was abandoned by his accomplices? Rick said he was shot, but there was no apparent wound. Was that a lie too?

Hank asked Rick to join him in an empty treatment room just off the ER. Rick wore a set of green hospital scrubs because his own clothing was covered in blood when he got to the hospital. Unbeknownst to Rick, his clothes were now secured in a bag sealed with a label that read "Evidence." Hank sat on the bed and offered Rick the bedside chair. That meant Hank sat above Rick, in a dominant position. He asked Rick to tell him what occurred step-by-step. Hank knew that the story Rick would tell would either make him a victim or an accomplice to robbery, kidnapping and attempted murder—or worse if Fabby died.

After Rick finished describing the entire incident, Hank got him a Coke from the nearby vending machine. Such a gesture would make a suspect believe that Hank bought his story hook, line and sinker. That is exactly what Hank wanted him to think as he started to ask Rick more pointed questions about the robbery and shooting. Starting from the conclusion of events and working back to the beginning, Hank looked for contradictions in Rick's recitation of the events. By changing the sequence of events, if there were lies being told, they should become evident because most people memorize their lies from start to finish.

After fifty minutes, Hank could not shake the kid's story. That was when Hank asked to see Rick's stomach. What he saw was puzzling, even to the veteran of many gunshot cases. A streak of skin across Rick's waist was red. The streak extended an inch to either side of his navel.

"Are you sure you were shot?" the detective asked.

"I thought so," Rick said. "I turned and saw Fabby fall. I heard the gun fire and felt a pain in my gut and fell to the ground."

About that time, Lenny came into the room and saw in Hank's eyes that he was unsure of Rick's role in the crime. As Hank was about to turn Rick over to the onslaught he knew Lenny would unleash, he thought, could this nice kid be a victim of falling in with a bad crowd?

Before Hank finished the thought, Lenny reported, "The kid's clean. His story checks out."

Lenny, who had been in contact with the police officers who were interviewing Waldbaum's personnel, then told Hank, "Rick had no idea he would be the one accompanying Fabby to the bank tonight. The cashier made that decision five minutes before the bank drop. She told the uniform officers Rick could not have known he would be selected."

The theory that Rick would be able to coordinate a robbery in five minutes just didn't make sense. Hank was happy to hear the revelation.

Lenny then took the plastic evidence bag he was

holding and threw it on the bed. "Check out the belt buckle."

Hank reached into the bag and found a wide leather belt crusted with blood.

As the buckle end of the belt emerged, Hank realized what occurred on Bagatelle Road. The buckle was wide, made of heavy metal. It had a chunk of metal gouged out, matching the bruise on Rick's stomach. The bullet fired at Rick hit his belt buckle and ricocheted off. The fact that Rick wasn't wounded was indeed a miracle. Now they only needed one more miracle—for Fabby.

It was 5:15 a.m. Sunday morning when Betty Budzick was awaken by her doorbell ringing again and again. At the door was uniformed Nassau Police Officer Murray Silverman.

"What happened?" Betty asked. She was half asleep but concerned that a family member may have been in an auto accident. Officer Silverman assured her that everything was all right and that he just wanted to talk to her about a stickup at the Waldbaum's last night. Those words jolted Betty out of the remnants of her sleep. As the officer started asking his prepared list of questions, Betty left him standing in her hallway and ran directly to the kitchen. The stunned Silverman followed her and observed her inexplicably digging through her trash bin. Then she handed him a brown Waldbaum's grocery bag.

"That was the plate number of the suspicious Corvair I saw in the parking lot," Betty said.

Silverman knew he had hit pay dirt. He had not told

Betty anything about the car used in the hold up, but she knew its model and had its license plate number. She also described the two suspicious men in detail, especially the one with the rodent-like features. When Officer Silverman asked her to explain what she meant by that, Betty described the man as having "a prominent overbite, a pointed chin and close-set eyes."

It did not take the police long to identify the registered owner of the gray 1966 Corvair bearing tag SKJ-7419 as one Anthony Pusateri of Flushing in Queens County. With the assistance of New York's Finest, Pusateri was arrested in his apartment on Franklin Avenue just off Main Street, without incident, and by 3:00 p.m., Anthony was comfortably seated in the robbery squad's office. Lenny and Hank were close to working a full twenty-four hours and had time for only a catnap while waiting for Anthony's arrival. As soon as they saw Anthony's beady eyes, overbite and pointed chin and nose, the detectives knew they had the man with rodent-like features as described by eyewitnesses Betty Budzick and Rick Cooper. That description fit Anthony Pusateri like a glove.

If I am completely truthful, the suspect didn't really sit "comfortably" in the interrogation room. More precisely, he sat in a metal chair with one loop of a handcuff on his wrist and the other end clasped around something you might see in a dungeon, a four-inch-diameter ring bolted to the room's wall.

Another robbery squad detective told Lenny and Hank to take a break while he processed Pusateri. The detective then placed a police form in the IBM Selectric typewriter and proceeded to get Anthony's pedigree—name, date of birth, address, employment, scars, etc. The two-finger typing of the detective would drive any typist insane, but finger by finger, correct-a-tape by correct-a-tape, the form was filled out. Then, it was off to fingerprints and photographs. Anthony's fingers were covered with black ink and the detective meticulously rolled each finger to get a clear print. With a set of clear prints sent to NYSIS in Albany, the department would get the suspect's RAP sheet.

The traditional mug shot followed next. About two hours later, Pusateri was placed in a lineup and was positively identified by Rick as the driver of the car. Then it was off to a holding cell.

Lenny had gotten his second wind. He showered and shaved at the squad and then combed back his black hair. He was ready to speak *to* Anthony. There would be little speaking at the start *by* Anthony. Lenny began with the terms "armed robbery," "kidnapping," "attempted murder" and "murder," if Fabby should die.

"You're toast, Anthony," Lenny yelled. "You give us the shooter, or you go down for the rap alone."

Before long, Anthony's enlightened self-interest prevailed, and he gave Lenny the name and address of his friend, Jimmy Panone.

"Why did you two not just take the money and leave the guys by the bank?" Hank asked.

Anthony's response was chilling, even to the detectives.

"Jimmy's nuts and … a killer. I just wanted my share of the take. It was his idea to kill the guys."

I never got the story on how Hank and Lenny apprehended Jimmy, so I guess it was rather routine once

Anthony gave up his accomplice.

I first met Jimmy when he was assigned to Legal Aid as a client charged with two counts of attempted murder, first-degree robbery, second-degree kidnapping and assorted other charges. While it was evident that Panone intended to kill both men from the time they were forced into the Corvair, he did not finish the job. With four rounds left in his revolver, he could have easily approached the bodies of his fallen victims and made sure of the kill with a round into each of their skulls. Why he did not, was anybody's guess. Perhaps, it was the answer to the prayers Fabby was saying during the short car ride.

It was the first week of October when Peter Lazarus, the senior Legal Aid trial attorney, was formally assigned to represent Jimmy Panone. I had been on the job about a month, waiting to be admitted to the bar in January and doing all sorts of scut work, mostly legal research. The staff trial attorneys were just too busy handling cases to conduct extensive research on issues that might help them at trial. That's where the intern (I) came in. I spent 90 percent of my day in the library, which was not my concept of what a trial attorney does. That was about to change. Peter called me into his office and commandeered me. I was to stop all other work because I was now the intern on the biggest case in the office, the Panone case. My first assignment was to read all the information we had on the case and study the notes Peter had taken during his two previous interviews with the client. It was my job to follow up on open questions that Peter wanted addressed. That meant I would sit down with Panone myself.

I was thrilled to escape the library and was so focused on understanding what Peter needed me to do in my interview with Panone that two things did not cross my mind until I reached Nassau County Jail. First, I had been to the jail twice before, shadowing one of our attorneys, but this was my first solo run. Second, in about ten minutes, I would be face-to-face in a small room with a killer. Fabby and Rick were alive, but that didn't alter the fact that Panone was willing to kill them.

Just getting into the attorney interview area at the jail was a bit unnerving for a rookie. I signed in at the front desk, showed my ID and waited for the correction officer to open the door. He used a metal key about five inches long that looked like a movie prop, but it opened the steel door. My briefcase and my person were hand searched, and I was directed down a flight of stairs to another steel door. A video camera announced my presence to the control room on the other side. I stood facing the door until I heard the electric lock snap open, which was the cue to enter.

I found myself in an area twice the size of a four-car garage. This was where the jail's buses and cars enter to take prisoners to court. A floor-to-ceiling gate ran fifteen feet wide and separated me from the corridor prisoners came down to get onto their transport. I waved to the correction officer on the other side, and half of the gate slid to the right. I entered and walked down a corridor to a similar gate fifty feet away. Holding cells lined both sides of the corridor, but they were empty.

As I got halfway down the corridor, I heard the clank of

55

the gate closing behind me. The sound echoed in my ears (and it's a sound I can still hear as I write this).

When I reached the second gate, another officer approached me, took his five-inch key off a metal ring on his belt and opened the door. I was in.

I gave him the name of the client I wanted to see. The correction officer escorted me to one of eight interview rooms. Each one was three and a half feet long by four feet wide and furnished with a small metal table and two metal chairs. The rooms were constructed of cinder block and had thin metal doors. The doors provided privacy but were thin enough for correction officers to breech in case an attorney's interview got out of control.

I didn't know what to expect when I met Jimmy Panone. Peter had told me that Jimmy was low key and appreciated that we were helping him. Peter had met murderers before. My only exposure to criminals had been dealing with speeding tickets. I started to rehearse for the hundredth time what to say when I first met Jimmy. I had a mental image of the kind of person who has the ability to take another's life.

When he came into the small room, I stood to introduce myself, and we shook hands. There I was, holding the hand of a man who fired a gun at two innocent supermarket workers with one intent—and that was to kill them in cold blood. Maybe it was my imagination, but I swear I could feel the temperature in the room noticeably drop.

During a forty-minute interview, Panone was polite but did not show any emotion about what happened that day. He answered the questions I was told to ask and a few follow up questions that I ad-libbed. I'm no psychiatrist, but

Jimmy displayed all the signs I had read about indicating he was a psychopath. He was devoid of all emotion and displayed no sorrow or conscience while we spoke of the armed robbery, kidnapping and attempted murder. It was almost like he was just an observer to what happened, not the main character in the drama.

Working for Lazarus was going to be difficult but was worth the cost. Peter was Legal Aid's top gun, a tough former Marine who still wore his hair cropped close, even in the days when long hair was fashionable. He was a skilled and seasoned trial attorney and insisted on people who worked with him being well prepared.

Lazarus's rule was as simple as it was difficult. "Fully prepare the case for trial, and then when done, prepare it again." He truly believed in the old military axiom "prior planning prevents poor performance." Since the attempted murder and robbery trial was going to be a hard-fought battle, especially in light of the evidence against Panone, Peter wanted the best investigator Legal Aid had on the case, so he hand-picked Eddie Karam.

Eddie was an ex-street cop from Brooklyn. Legal Aid employed four other investigators, all of whom had retired from the New York City Police Department with the gold shield bearing the word "Detective." Eddie, on the other hand, did all his time on the force in the bag (the police uniform). He never made the coveted rank of detective, but Eddie had the unique ability to get everyone to open up and talk to him.

Standing five feet five, this rotund forty-seven-year-old

of Lebanese extraction was a Yogi Berra look-alike, with a big nose, deep-set dark eyes, and ears like radar dishes. You could not help but like Eddie. His use of "deezes" and "dozes," coupled with calling everyone "Cuz" (short for cousin), made you feel comfortable. Eddie did not judge a client; that was for the jury. His job was to get the facts and make the prosecution prove their case beyond a reasonable doubt.

Legal Aid needed its A-team because we were going against the boy wonder of the Nassau County District Attorney's Office, Deputy Homicide Chief Steve Sartori. The tall, lean, good looking Sartori gave the appearance of the all-American boy who would not prosecute anyone unless he was guilty beyond all doubt. Besides being a trial attorney just as skilled as Lazarus, Steve had a few other things going for him: the Nassau County Police Department and, in this case, the facts.

With the prospects of a major trial on the horizon, Peter and Eddie would get together daily and plan out the case strategy. I was relegated to doing the legal research, while the pros handled the trial tactics. Over the years, I would learn what they both already knew: the key to a good defense was to get as much information as possible as early as possible, thereby knowing well before the trial what the People's key witnesses would testify to. If you did that, you would be better able to poke holes in their testimony during cross-examination, hoping to create a reasonable doubt in the mind of at least one juror. The surest way to accomplish that goal was to interview the complaining witnesses.

Under New York law, the defense would not get

Fabby's or Rick's grand jury testimony or the statements they made to the police until *after* they testified at the trial. By then, our defense would be locked in, and we would not have adequate time to contradict any of their statements. But, if the witnesses could be interviewed ahead of time, we would be better able to adjust our strategy for jury selection, opening statement and the trial game plan. Eddie was the best at getting witness statements, and it was surprising to me how many complainants were willing to tell their story to the defendant's investigator. He came across as a kind and caring uncle, and that got witnesses, even victims of alleged rapes, to talk to him about the crime. While Eddie was very good, he struck out big time when he called Rick Cooper for an interview. After calling Rick's home and identifying himself as part of Panone's defense team, Rick politely refused but then firmly hung up on Eddie while he was in mid-sentence. When Eddie tried to contact Fabby, the response was much less than polite.

Peter's obsession to be totally prepared for trial made him nag at Eddie, and Eddie was going crazy because he could not get an interview with the two key witnesses against our client.

Then Eddie got an idea. It would be risky and very close to the legal and ethical lines, but Eddie felt it was worth the shot. Besides, if it worked, Eddie could get Peter off his back and let him concentrate on all the other attorneys screaming for his help on their cases. Eddie told Peter that the coming Sunday at about noon he would call the DiFrono's house and ask if they could see Fabby later that afternoon at about 3:00 p.m. Could Peter be available?

"Available?" Peter responded incredulously. "I would be available to speak to DiFrono on Mars. How the hell are you going to pull this off, Eddie?"

"Leave it to me, Cuz."

At noon on Sunday, Eddie called Fabby at his home.

"Mr. DiFrono? This is Eddie Karam of the Nassau County P.D. Can I stop by and see you this afternoon at three? It's about the Panone trial."

Jimmy Panone's trial was to start in two weeks, so Fabby readily agreed to the meeting. However, as Fabby thought more about the call, he did not recall the name Eddie Karam as being a detective assigned to the case. He had spoken to Lenny and Hank, of course, and also to two or three other police officers and a detective investigator at the DA's office.

Could that detective investigator have been this guy Karam? Fabby started to worry. Jimmy Panone, like Fabby, was of Italian extraction, and in the course of his lifetime, Fabby had run into a few Italian-Americans who were not exactly law-abiding citizens. Fabby had met a few people he could describe as Mafia types and his imagination started to get the best of him: What if Panone was somehow connected to some wise guys? Might he be able to get someone to do the hit that he so poorly executed that night on Bagatelle Road? "With me dead," Fabby thought, "Rick probably would be too scared to testify and the case against Panone would go down the drain."

After a few more moments of considering that dire possibility, Fabby reluctantly dismissed those thoughts and told himself, I watch too much TV. Nevertheless, as he sat down to watch the Giants v. Cowboys game, the call from Karam kept bothering him. After not being able to concentrate on the kickoff and the Giants' first defensive stand, he went to the bedroom and picked up the phone.

First, he called the robbery squad and was told that both Lenny and Hank were off duty. Then Fabby rummaged through a bunch of papers he kept in his nightstand until he found Lenny's business card. The card had the robbery squad number printed on its front, but even more importantly, what Fabby wanted was written in pencil on the back: Lenny's home number. Lenny was at his house having Sunday dinner with his in-laws when he got the call.

"Fabby, lock all the doors, and don't open them till I get there," he said as soon as Fabby told him about the call from Karam.

Lenny took off the dinner napkin that was still tucked into his shirt collar and called Hank.

"We don't have a Detective Karam on this case," Hank said.

"I'm going to Fabby's house. You call CPU and get us some artillery, just in case. We got an hour to be there by three."

———————

A little after 3:00 p.m., there was a knock on Fabby's front door. "Who's there?" Fabby asked.

"Hey, Mr. DiFrono, it's Eddie Karam from the Nassau County P.D."

"The door's open. Come in," Fabby said.

Eddie was ecstatic he was finally going to get his interview. He entered the house, followed closely by Peter, who had met him outside. It took Eddie about five paces into the DiFrono living room to realize something was very, very wrong. Peter did not have the same line of sight Eddie did and literally ran into him as Eddie stopped short and threw his hands high into the air.

Peter peered around Eddie to see that the DiFrono living room couch was at a forty-five-degree angle to the front door. The couch was turned around so the seat faced the door and a shotgun barrel appeared from each corner of the couch.

Before either Eddie or Peter could utter a sound, two men dressed in combat helmets and flak jackets emblazoned "POLICE" stood straight up. They pointed their shotguns at the intruders. The detectives rushed into the living room from the dining room and threw Peter and Eddie into the hallway wall. Hank took Eddie, and Lenny handled the larger Peter.

As Lenny slammed Peter into the wall, he thought, "I know this guy." After the pair were handcuffed and secured, it dawned on Lenny. "You're Peter Lazarus, Jimmy Panone's lawyer."

Sure, they knew each other. Peter spent the better part of a recent day cross-examining Detective Scuderi at a Wade hearing. The hearing was designed to assure that the procedures used in the mug shot array shown Fabby, from which he identified Jimmy as the shooter, and the lineup he organized for Rick's identification, complied with the law.

"What the hell are you two guys doing here?" Hank asked the obviously shaken investigator and lawyer.

"We just wanted to interview Mr. DiFrono and get his

side of the story," Eddie said sheepishly.

"And what's this Nassau County P.D. bullshit?" Lenny demanded.

"Nassau County Public Defender's office," Eddie said. The response drew a bit of laughter. Hank, Lenny, Peter and Eddie all knew that Nassau County Legal Aid never used the title "public defender," but that response by the gregarious Eddie broke the tension of the moment.

Lenny ordered the two members of the Nassau County "P.D." to be uncuffed. After discussing such topics as "impersonation of a police officer," "disbarment" and, of course, "you could have gotten your heads blown off," Lenny told them to get out of the house and leave Mr. DiFrono alone.

Although no charges were pressed by DiFrono or the police, Eddie and Peter had one hell of a dressing down by the chief attorney at Legal Aid, Jim Mulholland. The next day, the district attorney himself called Mulholland and demanded that Eddie and Peter be fired. If it were not for their longtime relationship and Steve Sartori's urging that firing Lazarus would only delay the start of the Panone case, the A-team would have been history. As far as Sartori was concerned, he could not believe the balls these two guys had in defending their client. While he knew he had the facts to convict Panone, he began to suspect that the trial would be a dog fight.

What Are the Odds

Although not as dramatic as the attempted interview of DiFrono, Eddie's interview of Jimmy's ex-girlfriend, Shirley Little, helped prove the truth in the old saying that it's a small world. Shirley told us that on the night of the Waldbaum's holdup, Jimmy had picked her up at the restaurant where she worked at about 11:30 p.m. From there, they went in her car to their usual motel in Amityville to spend the night. Since Jimmy had been out of work for nine months, Shirley usually paid the room charge. Not that night; Jimmy paid the bill in twenties. Later, when he took off his pants in their room, wads of tens and twenties fell out. Shirley knew better than to ask where the money came from.

When Eddie was about to leave after thanking her for her time, Shirley said that we should know one more thing.

She told Eddie that, four months after Jimmy's arrest, she had started dating a guy named Asher Richardson, and they planned to get married in December.

"Glad you're getting on with the rest of your life," Eddie responded.

"That's not all of it," Shirley said. "Asher is also going to testify at Jimmy's trial."

Seeing the confusion on Eddie's face, Shirley said, "Asher Richardson is the driver Rick Cooper flagged down on Bagatelle Road that night."

The Panone trial began in November 1972. By then, I was officially admitted to the bar and had my own case-load in district court, so I was not present during the trial. Nevertheless, I kept tabs on the proceedings each day by speaking to Eddie or Peter and pitching in as they requested. Although Peter and Steve fought like two gladiators in the coliseum, it did not take the jury long to convict Panone of attempted murder (two counts), second-degree kidnapping (two counts) and first-degree robbery.

At the time Jimmy was to be sentenced, I sat in the spectator section of Judge Douglas Youngman's courtroom. Judge Youngman was highly respected for his legal ability. He was a short, almost frail-looking man. Nevertheless, the scuttlebutt around the courthouse was that the front of his bench was padded with bullet proof material (true) and that Douglas Youngman was the best shot with a re-volver in the courthouse (probably true).

I sat in the middle section in the gallery, while Fabby DiFrono sat directly across the aisle. Lenny and Hank were there too. I knew both of them from the pretrial hearings when we struck up an acquaintance. It was during these hearings that Lenny showed me Rick Cooper's gouged out belt buckle, where the bullet meant to kill him had struck. When the detectives formally introduced Fabby to me, we shook hands but did not have a conversation. After hear-ing both Lazarus and Sartori on the issue of sentence, Judge Youngman asked if Jimmy wished to be heard. He did not. Then the judge sentenced Jimmy to a term not less than eight years or more than twenty-four years in state prison. Jimmy, who had been in jail from the moment of arrest, just shrugged and was led out of the courtroom by the sheriffs.

I thought that was the end of the drama. *Wrong.* As Peter and I walked out of the courtroom, Fabby DiFrono was waiting for us in the rotunda.

"Mr. Lazarus," Fabby called, "you are one miserable son of a bitch!"

Before Peter or I could react, he added "But if I ever get in trouble, I want you to be my lawyer."

Fabby held out his hand and complimented Peter on his tenacity. While Fabby was beaten up by Peter on the witness stand at the pretrial hearing and at trial, he was the kind of man who held no grudge. Well, almost.

As we three walked through the rotunda and down the courthouse steps, Fabby told us he was very happy that Jimmy got sent to jail, because if the judge had let him walk out of the courtroom, Jimmy would not have gotten very far. Fabby opened his sports coat jacket and showed us a scabbard under his arm. In the holster, he carried a Marine-issued KA-BAR combat knife, with its seven-inch clip point blade, which allowed for quicker and deeper penetration. In the days before metal detectors anyone could have brought anything into a courthouse.

"I'm an ex-Marine and current Italian. I know how to use this thing and would have if I had to."

Thank God, Fabby didn't have to.

Yes, Virginia, There Really
Is a HIPAA Police

All of the residents and interns at the hospital sat through mandatory training on the requirements of the Health Insurance Portability and Accountability Act of 1996, better known as HIPAA. Perhaps they had dozed through the three-hour lecture or, as people are inclined to do, thought the warnings had nothing to do with them. In any event, the experience did not prevent some of them from discussing the new patient in the hospital's VIP tower.

Like other world-class hospitals, Prestige University Medical Center, located in New York City, had special accommodations for celebrity patients ranging from rock stars to the leaders of foreign governments. Although these patients often checked in under assumed names, it would take no more than two nursing shifts to alert the entire hospital staff to the presence of a famous person. So it was with the new VIP patient.

From time immemorial, information shared between the patient and his or her physician has been held by the medical profession as confidential. The Hippocratic Oath contains that promise: *Whenever, in connection with my professional practice or not in connection with it, I see or hear, in the life of men, which ought not to be spoken of abroad, I will not divulge as reckoning that all such should be kept secret.*

Over the years, physicians, for the most part, honored their obligation, and the courts have consistently upheld the physician-patient privilege. Although patient confidentiality in the medical community was not broken, Congress decided to fix it with the passage of HIPAA. Whether the convoluted legislative language helped the situation or not is up for grabs. However, the one thing for certain was that a violation of the HIPAA regulations dealing with unauthorized access to a patient's identifiable health information would result in a fine of $1,000 to $50,000 and the potential for imprisonment for one year.

It was about 3:15 a.m. when the doctors' lounge on the tenth floor of Prestige Medical had its first visitor of the night, my soon-to be-client Samir Khan, MD. Dr. Khan was a third-year resident and the chief resident in the department of anesthesiology.

Prestige ran one of the best residency programs in the country, and Dr. Khan's outstanding academic record enabled him to be selected for this coveted position. Being the chief resident opened the door for Dr. Khan to be selected for an even more prestigious fellowship program at the University of Texas Health Science Center in Houston commencing the next year.

When an individual graduates from medical school and gets a doctor of medicine degree, that individual is still years off from becoming a physician in the truest sense of the word. Years of post-graduate training lie ahead: three years for a family practitioner or internist, five years to be a surgeon, up to seven if your goal is neurosurgery. The purpose of the residency program was to take the broad range of medical knowledge and basic clinical skills learned in med school and hone them in a particular subspecialty. The residents were taught by either the hospital's paid faculty or attending physicians.

The life of a resident is indeed a grueling one and traces its roots back to the days when young medical students actually lived in residence at the hospital and were on call all hours of the day and night. Eventually, it came to light that some programs so over-worked their residents that these sleep-deprived and over-taxed kids sometimes made life-threatening mistakes in judgment. In December 2008, the Accreditation Council for Graduate Medical Education recommended that residents work only eighty hours per week, take overnight shifts not more than one in three nights, work a shift no more than thirty consecutive hours and have at least ten hours off between shifts. Imagine working a thirty-hour shift, making decisions affecting another person's life and being badgered by attending physicians to do all manner of scut work, all while trying to learn your profession at the same time.

And you thought your job was stressful.

I tell you all of this because I want you to feel the pressure these residents in their mid-twenties were under day in and day out, and what it was like to be a resident in a high-powered program. Residents had to try to pass their rotations through the various medical specialties, to keep up with their class work and to try not to kill the patients they tended. I want you to feel all of that to appreciate what happened that night in the doctors' lounge.

———

In June 2010, I was in private practice and had extensive experience in representing physicians with issues concerning their licenses. One day, I took a phone call from a young man who was referred to me by an attorney in New York City. That young man was Samir Kahn.

Dr. Kahn was nervous during our initial telephone call. His breathing was rapid, and his words came out quickly. Anytime I asked him a question, he got more agitated, so I just let him take over and tell his story.

While Dr. Kahn's twenty-four-hour shift, from 11:00 p.m. to 11:00 p.m., began as hectically as usual, his early-morning workload took an unexpected and much appreciated downturn. It was one of those rare nights when the hospital, as he put it, "was quiet." Shortly after Dr. Khan entered the doctors' lounge, another third-year anesthesiology resident, two second-year internal medicine residents and a third-year surgical resident straggled in one by one. This gang of five was busy getting their mandatory cups of caffeine, and some even scanned the unhealthy vending machine offerings looking for a late-night snack.

While they took advantage of a little downtime, the residents engaged in shoptalk. Talking about their experiences was one way they learned their craft.

"Do you really think his penis curves to the left?" Dr. Jill Conway asked, in reference to the VIP on the tenth floor. She was the cute blonde internal medicine resident seated next to Dr. Khan.

"Of course it does," the surgical resident offered, "Everything about him goes to the left."

After a chuckle or two, Dr. Conway talked about her urology rotation, when she had occasion to observe a rare case of Peyronie's Disease. She then explained that the "*tunica albuginea* of the penis loses its elasticity and can cause a curvature to the right or left or up or down."

The surgical resident chimed in again and said that he doubted the diagnosis of Peyronie's, because such symptoms usually resulted from a trauma to the penis. Rather, he opined, the condition, if it existed at all, would be more likely to be a result of hypospadias, a condition in which a congenital defect resulted in the misplacement of the urinary opening.

The other residents now joined in, also challenging Dr. Conway's medical judgment, saying that they never saw or heard of such a condition and that Dr. Conway should "stop reading all those trashy tabloid" accounts of the VIP's sexual exploits.

Thus, what had started as a professional medical discussion had now degenerated into a full-blown twenty-minute argument culminating with the surgical resident, Dr. Bevilacqua, finally calling Jill a "blonde medical ignoramus."

Dr. Khan had been quietly sipping his coffee, watching his friends debate the medical conundrum until the five-foot-one Dr. Conway exploded to her feet to physically confront the six-foot male surgical resident, threatening him with a manual orchiectomy (look it up) then and there. To bring some order to the escalating chaos, Dr. Khan, invoking his position as the chief resident intervened, by literally jumping between his two colleagues and ordering: "Knock it off before you two wake up every patient in the hospital! I'm going to settle this issue once and for all. Jill, get his medical records up on the computer, so we can end this insanity."

Jill sat down in front of the computer, which had access to the medical records of every patient in the hospital. Her colleagues gathered about her. She duly entered her user ID and password. Then she typed in a name.

It was at this point Dr. Kahn interrupted his story to ask if I had any experience in defending HIPAA violations before the New York Office of Professional Medical Conduct (OPMC).[1] I told Dr. Khan that, while I have had more than my fair share of cases before OPMC, I never handled a HIPAA allegation as it was the federal Office of Civil Rights that investigates HIPAA violations.

In an effort to calm down the obviously agitated Dr. Khan, I quipped that I had yet to meet the HIPAA police.

"You may not have met them, but I sure have," was his terse response.

⎯⎯⎯ ⎯⎯⎯

Unbeknownst to Dr. Kahn, Dr. Conway and their nosey colleagues, just three floors above the doctors' lounge on

⎯⎯⎯⎯⎯⎯⎯⎯⎯⎯⎯⎯⎯

[1] OPMC is the branch to the New York Department of Health that investigates physicians accused of professional misconduct. If charges of professional misconduct are sustained, OPMC can take action against the physician's license to practice medicine. The sanctions can range from a confidential administrative warning all the way to a very public revocation of license.

the VIP floor of the hospital, another woman also sat in front of a computer. This woman, eight years senior to Dr. Conway, sat at a folding table that had been transformed into a communication center of sorts. Three telephones, white, blue and red in color, sat to her right. Her state-of-the-art laptop computer sat in the middle of the table, and a mobile radio base station with four handheld radios in their chargers was within reach of her left hand. The portable communication unit was set up quickly because the VIP's visit to the hospital had not been anticipated. Wires and cords that would have been properly cinched with color-coded tiebacks were left in what appeared to be a tangled spider's web.

Seven people attended the communications center and provided security for the VIP patient. Concetta Coraza, the junior member, had drawn the midnight-to-six watch. Four of her colleagues, including the team leader, slept in an adjoining room. Two others, also awake, sat just outside the patient's room.

When not on duty in their official business attire, the dress of the day consisted of black pants and matching shirt or the more fashionable black jumpsuit. Concetta opted for the jumpsuit. Concetta kept dipping a bag of chamomile tea into a mug (she hated coffee), thinking of almost anything to kill the boredom of being on watch. Sometimes being on watch was exciting, as when the area they were in could be deemed less than secure, but on this mid-February night in Prestige Medical, even without the assistance of New York's finest, she felt safe. She also thought back to her time in Quantico and how one of her instructors had described their job: 99 percent boredom and 1 percent sheer terror.

Then terror happened.

Seconds after Dr. Conway accessed the patient's medical record, a red light flashed repeatedly on Concetta's laptop, and an alarm buzzer sounded. Her training kicked in.

Without stopping to think, Concetta picked up the first radio on the console, pressed the send key and reported, "We have unauthorized access," to her team members in the patient's suite.

She then hit a second alarm button to wake her sleeping colleagues in the adjoining rooms and lifted the red phone off its cradle. The phone had a direct connection to the New York City Police Department's SWAT Team, the Emergency Service Unit.

"This is Candlestick. I need backup for EAGLE at his hospital suite."

"Affirmative" was the only response she received.

As the team leader shook the sleep out of her eyes, she ordered Concetta to "locate the point of access pronto."

Within seconds, Concetta had identified the point of the breach and the team was on the move "to the doctors' lounge on the tenth floor."

———

Dr. Khan continued with his story.

"We were huddled around Dr. Conway, who was seated at the computer scanning the patient's chart from his current admission and found nothing even to suggest her diagnosis of Peyronie's disease was correct. So we decided to dig deeper into his prior admissions and consultant reports. That's when it happened."

Dr. Khan's agitated voice was now trembling as he re-lived those moments in his mind's eye.

"All of a sudden, the door to the doctors' lounge was flung open, shattering the glass panel of the door. Five or six people all dressed in black charged into the lounge screaming at us at the top of their lungs, 'Show us your hands... Show us your hands... Get on the floor. Now.'

"As I turned towards the door, I saw the invaders. Each of them held what appeared to be a submachine gun, and the guns were pointed directly at us. We were ordered to get on the floor, face down, and those of us too stunned to move were forcibly thrown to the floor, including Dr. Conway, who sat frozen at the computer.

"Once I was on the floor, I felt a knee in my back and my arms were pinned behind me and secured with plastic ties. When I looked to my left, I saw a woman with her machine gun within two feet of my head. They continued yelling and screaming at us not to move. I thought they were terrorists and they were going to execute us then and there.

"After being on the floor for what seemed like an hour but was probably only five minutes, I saw the blue uni-forms of the New York City Police Department in full combat gear appear at the door to the lounge. I was never so happy to see a policeman. Then I thought we would be caught in the crossfire between the police and the in-vaders. However, instead of bullets being fired, the first few cops that came into the room just looked around and laughed.

"It took another few minutes for the administra-tor-on-call to arrive, and by then, we'd been pulled to sitting positions in a circle in the middle of the room. Then, one by one, we were identified by the administrator as hospital residents. As the administrator continued making his identifications, the machine guns were slowly placed in the invaders' shoulder holsters, but their hands still rested on the butt of the pistols they wore on their thighs. We were told to sit quietly and then were taken one by one into a room across the hall. We were still handcuffed. The woman who appeared to be the leader interrogated us separately. The question was, why were we accessing a patient's medical records without a medical reason? After we were interrogated, we went back to the lounge, this time without our handcuffs, and were told to take a seat and wait for the director of the residency program to arrive.

"Other residents and staff started to gather in such numbers that the university police had to cordon off the area from our nosey colleagues. Then the invaders in black vanished as quickly as they appeared.

"While the incident seemed funny to some of the SWAT officers who were still in the room watching over us, the director of the program did not find any of this humorous.

"'You violated HIPAA,' he shouted three or four times. He told us we were not only a disgrace to Prestige Medical but to the very profession of medicine itself. The director saved most of his angry words for me because I was the senior physician in the group, and I was the one who suggested we look at the patient's records. He then proceeded to take each of our hospital ID cards and suspended us for two weeks without pay. We were also told to report to the chief operating officer's office at 9:00 a.m. sharp.

"At that meeting, the COO said he should throw us out of the program for the embarrassment we caused the hospital. However, due to some intervention far above him, and against his better judgment, he was only adding an additional week to our previously issued suspension and ordering a full-day HIPAA seminar as a precondition to our return to the program.

"Lastly, he said that Prestige Medical was notifying OPMC as required by law for 'whatever action they wished to take against our licenses.'

"That's why I am calling you," Dr. Khan ended.

After telling his story, Dr. Khan asked if I could represent all the residents before OPMC, as individually they would not be able to afford my fee. I told Dr. Khan that I would be glad to do so, if all the prospective clients agreed to waive any conflict of interest concerns. Also, before being retained on this matter, I would have to be assured that OPMC would not object to this representation. To clear that hurdle, I needed to call the agency's executive secretary, who I had met several times. The executive secretary was both a physician and a lawyer and had a reputation of being both mean-spirited and arrogant.

He seemed to relish lambasting doctors who came before him for a confidential administrative warning. If a physician was lucky enough to convince the OPMC director that his conduct did not rise to a level of professional misconduct, but was merely questionable, a confidential administrative warning would be issued to that physician. That procedure required the physician to meet the executive secretary in a face-to-face meeting. At this meeting,

"Doctor-Doctor," as we called him because of his double degrees, took great pleasure in berating the offending physician in a less than professional tone and in less than professional language more befitting a truck driver than a physician.

I got the executive secretary on the phone and began to explain the reason for my call. About one minute into my recitation of the case, he interjected.

"Gregg, stop. I know all about it."

Specifically, he said that OPMC was aware of the fact that Prestige Medical had suspended all of the residents for three weeks without pay and prescribed additional HIPAA training for each of them. Uncharacteristically, he chuckled and offered, "You know, I've heard that there were yellow stains on some of those white hospital uniforms after they got done with them."

In short, he stated that the residents had learned their HIPAA lesson as very few have. He then assured me that OPMC would take no further action against the residents. His decision shocked me. I had expected him to jump all over me and my case, but instead I conveyed my clients' gratitude for OPMC's understanding.

Living up to his reputation of being a class A SOB (which does not stand for the medical abbreviation, Short Of Breath), Doctor-Doctor said that the residents did not have the brains God gave the geese and if it was up to him, he would have placed the entire crew on probation for three years as they were a disgrace to the profession, but "the decision was taken out of my hands."

Epilogue

That concluded the matter. The residents took their suspension and the all-day HIPAA seminar (more than a sufficient penalty, to say the least) and returned to completing their program. While there may, in reality, be no HIPAA police, the residents learned that before you go wandering through a person's medical record, you must have a *bona fide* medical reason. Jill Conway should have known that before she typed in the letters of the patient's name:

W-i-l-l-i-a-m J-e-f-f-e-r-s-o-n C-l-i-n-t-o-n.

～ 4 ～

Doctor Chang's OOPS

"They can't take my husband's medical license. We have two children to support, and besides, he's not guilty." Annette Chang, the wife of my client Daniel Ho Chang, MD, had a shrill voice and used it. I acknowledged that she had reason to worry.

In ten days, at the Office of Professional Medical Conduct (OPMC) in Albany, that crucial decision about her husband's career would be made in a hearing before a panel of two physicians and a layperson.

Doctors get hauled before OPMC when they are charged with an act of professional misconduct or convicted of a crime. Generally, before a doctor gets to a hearing, formal charges have been filed by the State Health Department against the physician and all attempts to negotiate a settlement of the charges have failed. The stakes at most hearings are extraordinarily high. The department always seeks revocation of the doctor's license, while the defense usually argues for a stayed suspension which allows the doctor to continue his practice on probation and with the doctor's medical care periodically reviewed by a practice monitor. As precious few hearings ever resulted in an outright win for the doctor, I always tried to negotiate a settlement on the eve of trial. However, this case was different. The department sought to revoke the doctor's license and would not consider any other penalty because the doctor pled guilty to "that crime."

As with most of my cases, nothing was simple. Yes, my client, Dr. Daniel Chang, pled guilty to the commission of a crime, but it was a strange crime indeed and had absolutely nothing to do with the practice of medicine. As the doctor's guilt was already established by his guilty plea in criminal court, the only thing I could do was present a good enough argument to mitigate the severity of the punishment.

My firm had not handled Dr. Chang's criminal case, and I was told no health law attorney had been consulted by his defense counsel. Counsel either was unaware or did not care about the collateral damage a physician would suffer as a result of the guilty plea; he just knew a good plea bargain when he was offered one. Specifically, the doctor's criminal conviction would not only put his license at risk, but it also endangered his hospital admitting privileges and his participation in various health insurance plans, which generally account for the bulk of a doctor's income. Although Dr. Chang was originally charged with a class A misdemeanor, which carries up to one year in jail, his counsel was given the opportunity to have him plead to the lesser charge of a class B misdemeanor, the lowest type of crime in the state penal law. To sweeten the plea deal, the DA agreed to a sentence of a conditional discharge, which put Dr. Chang on unsupervised probation for one year. If he did not commit another crime during that year, his sentence would be deemed satisfied. From a criminal law practitioner's viewpoint, it was a great disposition, especially considering the facts of the case.

Although Doctor Chang steadfastly maintained he was not guilty of any crime, he didn't want to suffer the expense of paying an attorney or the time he would lose from his practice by going to trial. Hence, he decided to take the easy way out and get the criminal matter behind him in one court appearance. It was now my task to convince three sane and rational people why my client should continue to treat patients at his sole practice of neurology when he stood convicted of "that crime."

What was the crime, you ask? Here are the facts that led to the criminal conviction, so you can decide how you would present the case to the hearing panel.

One day, Dr. Chang found himself in Father Duffy's Square, located at Broadway and Forty-Seventh Street in Manhattan, looking to purchase discounted play tickets for that evening's performance of *Monty Python's Spamalot*. Dr. Chang saw a large group of people forming a block away. This group was gathering to hear a rock band play a few of their hits in the middle of Times Square. As a self-described connoisseur of music ranging from classical to heavy-metal, the doctor followed the music and joined the crowd.

Unfortunately for the doctor, while he was standing in the crowd, his penis inexplicably escaped from his trousers. More unfortunately and just as inexplicably, his liberated penis found its way to rubbing against the rather large buttocks of a female. To compound his misfortune, it was later determined that the violated booty belonged to a thirteen-year-old.

This string of just downright bad luck culminated when

two people approached Dr. Chang and gave him two pieces of friendly advice: "Put your dick back into your pants," and "Put your hands behind your back." With the latter command, the two undercover police officers monitoring the crowd made an unexpected arrest. That's New York City for you… just full of surprises.

It was Dr. Chang's plea to the class B misdemeanor of sexual abuse in the third degree that would take us to the OPMC hearing. In retrospect, had defense counsel contacted a health law attorney, the suggestion of pleading the doctor guilty to a different class B misdemeanor, such as public lewdness or exposure of a person, would have been made. While the criminal outcome would remain the same for Dr. Chang, the optics of the case would have been better for the OPMC presentation. It was bad enough to have a doctor who exposed himself, but that could be characterized as a personal problem to be dealt with via psychotherapy; much worse to have a client who was convicted of sexual abuse of an underage girl. The hearing panel would not want such a doctor alone with a patient in a small examination room. In short, the panel would not want to take the responsibility if something untoward should occur in the future. It was much easier to do the CYA thing and revoke his license.

In preparation for my last meeting with Dr. Chang before the hearing, I phoned the OPMC prosecutor in a last-ditch attempt to save the doctor's license before the hearing started. While generally polite, the prosecutor reiterated that the health department would accept no resolution of this case short of Dr. Chang surrendering his medical license. If we failed to do so, the department would move to revoke his medical license at the hearing. This was truly a Hobson's choice. Either way, the doctor would lose his license and not be able to practice. While the surrender of the license might be favorable from a strategy posture when he reapplied for his license in five years, it was not a realistic option. However, there was a strategy we could employ at the hearing that just might convince the hearing panel that Dr. Chang was not a danger to the community. The doctor and I had previously agreed on this tactic, and we were at this meeting to finalize our strategy.

Without any advance notice to me, Dr. Chang brought a guest with him to this meeting, his wife, Annette. They made a strange couple. Dr. Chang stood five feet, five inches tall, was a bit overweight and always had a smile on his round face. Annette presented the opposite. She was five feet, ten inches tall, very thin, wore her long black hair in a hippie-like fashion and displayed a countenance between arrogance and annoyance. She never smiled. While Dr. Chang had always taken an active role in our discussions, the presence of Annette made him take a backseat.

Annette announced that she was admitted to the New York State bar after graduating *cum laude* from Columbia University Law School. She then worked for eight months as an associate in the mergers and acquisitions department of a major Wall Street firm until she chose the higher profession of being a stay-at-home mom to the couple's four-year-old twin girls and working part time at Dr. Chang's solo neurology practice. Although Annette had never set foot in a courtroom, she decided that she should direct the strategy for her husband's hearing. Her sole contribution to this effort was this: "My husband did not do anything wrong." Apparently, Annette was absent from her criminal law course the day the professor stated the legal principle that a plea of guilty was the same as a conviction after trial.

No matter how I tried to reason with her, she always responded that her husband was innocent. After an hour passed, my Italian temper got the best of me, and I advised the doctor I would be happy to withdraw from the case and have his wife represent him. Dr. Chang then woke up from his apparent stupor and had a one-word comment: "No." Not to be deterred, Annette said she would be coming to the hearing.

On the day of the hearing, the proceedings commenced at 2:00 p.m. I generally preferred to have the 10:00 a.m. hearing slot, but that would require that we (Chang, Annette and I) would go to Albany (a four-hour drive) the night before and have dinner and a short prep. I could not bring myself to have dinner and an argument with the know-it-all Annette before the hearing, so I opted for the later time and we drove up separately. As I anticipated when we met at 1:00 p.m., I barely got my coat off before Annette barraged me with her new analysis of the case and updated trial strategy. This was going to be a long day.

The hearing panel consisted of two physicians, a middle-aged internist and a older disheveled psychiatrist, and was chaired by a non-medical member of the state board of medicine. As the prosecutor finished his opening statement, Annette handed me several notes on how I should respond. I ignored her suggestions and began my opening.

Not more than thirty seconds into it, the psychiatrist

stood up and shouted, "I'm sorry."

We all looked at him quizzically as he fumbled through a stack of papers on the table in front of him and reported that it just dawned on him that he had been on the OPMC panel that voted for charges against Dr. Chang and by law could not sit on the penalty panel. Why it took this physician so long to realize he had previously adjudicated a case with this bizarre fact pattern is unknown. The one thing that was known was the hearing could not proceed and it was adjourned for one month, which meant one more month of dealing with the woman I now thought of as the Wicked Witch of Staten Island.

Annette continued to hound me for the next several weeks, even after I sent her the transcript of her husband's plea before the judge in which Dr. Chang admitted, under oath, that on the day in question, he rubbed his penis against the buttocks of a female, but he did not know she was under fourteen. I also told her that the OPMC does not retry the underlying case. All the panel was permitted by law to do was to decide on a penalty for his conviction of a crime. I continued to tell Annette that if Dr. Chang now testified under oath that he did nothing wrong, he would be either admitting to perjury before the criminal court judge or to perjury before the hearing panel. I concluded by saying that it was their choice on how to proceed; either way, the panel had Dr. Chang in an untenable position. Eventually, Annette agreed to stay out of the trial strategy, but wanted input on the penalty we would recommend the hearing panel impose.

At the start of the second hearing, the prosecutor, as anticipated, introduced a certified copy of Dr. Chang's conviction to the crime of sexual abuse in the third degree, a class B misdemeanor, as well as Dr. Chang's sworn plea allocution before the court. He then sat down.

Contrary to Annette's wishes, my strategy was not to have Dr. Chang renounce his plea. The panel most likely would not believe him, and it would be disastrous for them to think he was lying now, which I believed would definitely ensure the revocation of his license. I had Dr. Chang acknowledge he took the plea and explain that he did so to avoid a trial, which would have cost him $2,500 in legal fees and significant loss of time from his solo practice. I thought this would resonate with the two physicians on the panel, both solo practitioners themselves. I reiterated that a plea to a class B misdemeanor was the lowest crime available in the penal law and that the sentence of conditional discharge was the lowest sentence that could be imposed by the court. Additionally, I introduced five affidavits from prominent physicians who spoke of Dr. Chang's outstanding medical skills and his good reputation in the Staten Island medical community. I introduced five more affidavits from current patients, all of whom spoke to his professional care and concern for them in dealing with their medical problems. Each said they would continue to have Dr. Chang as their neurologist and three said they would have no difficulty in having him treat their minor children.

A recess was then declared, and the panel advised that when we returned, they wanted to hear our summations, as well as our proposals for the penalty to be imposed.

During the break, Dr. Chang, Annette and I huddled, and I reiterated my decision to propose a penalty of a fine and a three-year license suspension, fully stayed (which would allow the doctor to continue to practice) on the condition that Dr. Chang be accompanied by a female chaperone any time he treated a female patient under the age of eighteen. The doctor weighed the options. I personally thought I was asking a lot of the panel but wanted to give it a try. Of course, Annette disagreed, saying she wanted a confidential administrative warning, the lowest penalty the panel could impose. I told her the panel would never go for her suggestion because they would be worried about the bad publicity OPMC would receive if Dr. Chang inappropriately touched a minor patient in the future.

Nevertheless, Annette said her main concern was the cost of hiring an additional staff person to act as a chaperone for the few minor patients the doctor saw. I was shocked at Annett's position, since they had known for weeks that I would be seeking a stayed suspension with a chaperone being present for minor patients. We then renewed our verbal spat, with me saying she was being penny-wise and pound-foolish risking her husband's license for a few dollars to pay for a chaperone and she saying we did not have the balls to ask for complete vindication. How could anyone think that the New York State Department of Health would vindicate one of their physicians who pleaded guilty to the crime of sexual abuse on these facts involving an underage female? I was convinced Annette had lost her mind.

I had had it with Annette and declared that she and Dr. Chang had five minutes to decide what they wanted to do. They could take my advice, which had a slim chance of succeeding, or roll the dice that Annette was holding.

Perhaps it was the first time Dr. Chang stood up to his domineering wife. He decided that half a loaf was better than trying to support his family in an occupation other than the practice of medicine.

Annette was visibly angry with both of us. She sat at our table with arms folded and had the face of a four-year-old about to have a temper tantrum. When I made our recommendation to the panel, she intentionally knocked her pocketbook to the floor with a loud thump to note her objection. She left the hearing room without saying goodbye to me, although Dr. Chang extended his hand and said thanks.

Three weeks later, the panel voted unanimously to impose a $10,000 fine and a five-year suspension of Dr. Chang's license, fully stayed with the condition that a chaperone be present for the examination of minor children. Dr. Chang's license was saved.

A week later, I got a handwritten thank you note signed, "With appreciation and love, Annette."

—5—

The Book of Francis

A solitary plaque adorns the drab institutional-green walls of the lobby of a certain prosecutor's office. Hundreds of employees have passed through the lobby's doors in the forty-plus years of its existence, but there is only one person honored with a plaque. It is there not because the recipient was killed in the line of duty or performed some heroic act; it is there because the recipient was an outstanding individual who, in his own unique way, taught young men and women how to become investigators. Moreover, he was simply a man loved by those who worked with him. I remember Francis Brennan well, with his shock of white hair, round face and piercing blue eyes, almost hidden by his tinted spectacles.

Francis Brennan, the son of Irish immigrant parents, not only became a member of New York's Finest but also retired with the rank of detective first grade, an elite designation for the department's most senior and experienced investigators. Notwithstanding his exceptional career in the tough police precincts of Brooklyn, Francis was most proud of his only son, a Roman Catholic priest.

When it came to being a cop, Francis himself was far from priestly. He was tougher than nails one moment yet could become the kindly old professor the next. He taught book-smart, just-out-of-college investigators the street smarts they needed. Francis taught by relating parables, just as in the Gospels, imparting to his young students the knowledge acquired from his successes, as well as his failures. These were lessons that could only be taught by someone who had experienced them. Whether Francis's parables were factually accurate was not the issue. Rather, it was the lessons the parables taught that was important.

⌒ Parable 1: The Call Box ⌒

This parable drew from Francis's own first weeks as a New York City policeman. His first assignment fresh out of the academy was to a precinct in the heart of a commercial area off Atlantic Avenue and Court Street in downtown Brooklyn. Because he was the precinct's rookie, he drew the graveyard shift, walking a beat from 11:00 p.m. until 7:00 a.m.

It was early fall, and Francis was decked out in his crisp new blue uniform. A .38-caliber revolver hung on his right hip, and his new twenty-three-inch nightstick hung on his left. During his beat, Francis was to check the retail establishments for signs of trouble. He would peer into the storefront windows in hopes of spotting a burglary in progress. But even Francis realized that such an event was unlikely. Rather, he made sure the merchants had locked their front door or secured the iron gates protecting their property.

After several weeks, walking the beat became boring to the point that Francis spent a good deal of time practicing twirling his nightstick like the old-timers.

Francis would start his beat when a radio car dropped him off at Call Box 31. Rookies were not assigned to radio cars. They had to earn that privilege by pounding the beat for several years. The call box in front of Francis was a green rectangular box with the word "POLICE" emblazoned on its front, five feet and six inches off the ground and mounted on a telephone pole. Once opened, the call box revealed a phone, which connected to the front desk at the Eighty-Third Precinct. Francis followed a simple procedure. At the start of the beat, he called the desk sergeant from Call Box 31 and advised him he was commencing his tour. Francis then walked the twenty-six blocks to the end of the beat and checked in with the precinct by using Call Box 28 to report any incidents and his location. In the days before cell phones and personal police radios, the call box was the only way the precinct could keep track of their officers and make sure they were safe.

After hanging up with the desk officer from Box 28, Francis crossed over to the opposite side of the street, continuing to check storefronts and door locks, on his way back to Call Box 31.

The brisk fall weather that originally invigorated Francis for his midnight walk soon turned into a biting winter wind. On one particular night, the wind was nothing compared to the freezing rain that pelted the rookie. He could fight the wind, but when the wind-driven sleet struck his face, it stung like a hundred bees circling his head. After three hours in the inclement weather, Officer Brennan made a decision.

From his time working in the station house, Francis

knew that whether you called in from Box 31 or Box 28, the same light would glow on the station's switchboard. Therefore, the desk sergeant had no independent way of verifying the caller's location and relied solely on the officer's verbal representations.

This night, Francis called in from Box 28 and reported he was heading up the avenue to Box 31 and hung up. But he didn't head that way. Having walked the beat for several months, Francis knew well which storefront he could duck into and, as they say in police jargon, "coop" out of the wind and sleet. He let about fifteen extra minutes pass from his usual call-in time at Box 31. He thought it made sense that additional time would be needed to get to the call box on this hellish night. The parable continues.

Precinct: Eighty-Third Precinct, Officer Kyle O'Ryan speaking.

Brennan: Kyle, this is Brennan. I am at Box 31. It's now zero two hundred hours.

Precinct: Confirm. Officer Brennan, Box 31, zero two hundred hours.

As Francis was about to hang up, the desk officer said, "Brennan, hold on. Sergeant Radigan wants to speak to you."

Francis tried to catch his breath. Sergeant Sean Radigan was the top sergeant at the Eight-Three. With over thirty years on the job, the precinct captain let him do pretty much what he wanted. Moreover, since Sean's brother was Monsignor Timothy Radigan, secretary to the beloved cardinal of New York, Sergeant Radigan could do no wrong in the eyes of the police commissioner, and more importantly, in the eyes of the mayor. (Indeed, the relationship between the two members of the cloth was so close that it was commonly joked that Monsignor Radigan was the "cardinal's left ball.")

All of the patrol officers, especially the rookies like Francis, knew that the support of Sergeant Radigan was critical to their future promotions. Being in such a position of power, Radigan took it upon himself to become the precinct's training officer so he could spot up-and-coming patrolmen.

Radigan, who spoke with a very thick Gaelic brogue, picked up the phone.

Radigan: Francis, me lad, how are you holding up on this hellish night?

Brennan: Doing OK, Sarge. It's freezing, but I love doing my job.

Radigan: Glad to hear you're so dedicated. You are going to make your parents proud of their son and become a fine police officer.

Then, almost as an afterthought, Radigan said, "By the way, son, where are you located?"

Brennan: At Box 31, Sarge, and I am heading back to 28.

Radigan: Fine laddie, but before you go, I know you're a smart young man, and I have just one question for ya.

Brennan: Sure, Sarge.

Radigan: Francis, I want you to spell a word for me. The word is apothecary.

Brennan: Apothecary?

Radigan: Yes, lad … apothecary. It's another word for a

pharmacy. Now, spell it.

Brennan: A-P-O-T-E…

Radigan: Wrong, Francis. Do it again.

Brennan: A-P-O-H…

Radigan (interjecting and getting angry): Wrong again.
Francis, if you're at Box 31 and if you look across the
street at the third store from the corner on your left,
you will see Ashworth's Apothecary. Now, spell it.

Brennan: … (silence)

Radigan: I thought so. Now get your fat, dumb Irish ass
down to Box 31, and if you ever pull that shit on the
department again, I will make bloody sure you spend
the rest of your career walking the zoo beat at Central
Park.

Fifty-five minutes later, when Officer Francis Brennan
called the precinct, Sergeant Radigan was waiting for the
call.

Radigan: Eight Three desk, Sergeant Radigan speaking.

Brennan: A-P-O-T-H-E-C-A-R-Y

Radigan: Well done, Francis.

So ends this parable.

LESSON LEARNED:
Never ever lie, especially to a superior.

⌇ Parable 2: The Flute ⌇

The next seven years of Francis's career saw some drastic changes take place in the department. Francis, who was now known as Frank, saw the "color barrier" into the Irish NYPD being regularly broken with the swearing in of Italian-American officers. Younger officers now got a chance to drive the radio patrol car in between shifts pounding the beat.

Frank was now studying for the sergeant's exam and was named a training officer for the new rookie class. Sergeant Radigan, older and crankier, was still the department's golden boy who could do no wrong. He took advantage of that blessing.

Radigan was no stranger at the local thirst shop after work, but over the years, had taken to having a nip or two even while on duty. To accomplish his extracurricular pop, Radigan used a flute—not the musical instrument, but rather a six-and-a-half-ounce contoured Coke bottle. If an officer paid a visit to McSorley's Old Ale House and said, "I'm here for Radigan's flute," Jake, the bartender, produced a Coke bottle filled with two shots of Jameson Irish Whiskey and three and a half ounces of Coke. The officer then delivered the resealed bottle to Radigan back at the station house.

Only a few cops in the precinct knew about the sergeant's flutes, and fewer still were entrusted with the task of delivering the item. Frank was one of the chosen few.

This day, Frank was to take his new recruit, Joe Pompei, to drive the sector near the Brooklyn waterfront. Pompei was a one-year member of the force, had walked his beat, and was transferred to the Eight-Three to replace an officer who had just retired. Pompei was assigned to work with Frank for two weeks in the sector's radio car to become familiar with his new precinct. Each radio car had two officers, the driver and the recorder. With Pompei behind the wheel, Car 111 left the precinct at 7:30 a.m.

In their first few days together, Frank had found that Pompei was a know-it-all about police work, even though he was still a rookie. He pontificated about any and all law enforcement topics and talked incessantly. Rather than listen, Frank tried to get a few winks while Joe drove.

As Car 111 left the precinct this fateful morning, Sergeant Radigan flagged it down. Officer Pompei dutifully stopped and cranked down the driver's side window. "Don't forget the flute on your way back this afternoon."

Radigan was directing his words to Frank in the passenger seat, but before Frank could respond, Pompei snapped, "Don't worry, Sarge. I'll personally take care of it," and he sped off.

Thirty minutes before the shift ended, Frank had had enough of Pompei's criticizing everything from the police department to the mayor and even Frank's beloved Dodgers.

Before Frank could tell the rookie to can it, Pompei hit the siren and, with flashing red lights, made a beeline across the Brooklyn Bridge to the Fulton Fish Market in lower Manhattan. Pompei screeched the squad car to a halt in front of the fish market and was out of the car in a flash. He ran into the market and ran back carrying a package.

"We will still make it back to the precinct on time."

Pompei was panting from his exertion. He tossed the bundle, an item wrapped in pages of the previous day's *Daily News* into Frank's lap. The item was cold and wet.

Perplexed, Frank sat quietly as the squad car, again with lights and siren blasting, headed across the bridge to the precinct. The light began to dawn on him, and he had to fight the urge to bust out laughing. Pompei was such a hump that Frank would not even think of helping him out, even though he knew there was an impending disaster in the making.

Five blocks from the station house, Pompei killed the siren and lights and drove slowly to the precinct's underground garage. Sergeant Radigan stood in the driveway, his hands clasped behind his back. Frank knew the drill. Once Radigan saw the car assigned to bring his flute approach, he would turn his back to the driver's side window. The driver would lower his window and make the handoff. Radigan would slip the flute into his pants pocket, and the driver would proceed to park the squad car.

This time, the drill was different. When Radigan held his hand behind his back for the transfer, he felt something long ... cold ... and wet.

He opened the newspaper wrapping to find a whole five-pound, fifteen-inch-long *fluke.*

Frank got out of the car and almost pissed in his pants when he saw Radigan running down the ramp into the garage holding the fish over his head like a club and yelling at Pompei, "You dumb Guinea bastard. I said 'flute' not 'fluke.'"

So ends this parable.

LESSONS LEARNED:
Fully understand your orders before you
undertake the assignment.

Never be ashamed to ask for help.

Don't act like you know everything
about a job you just started.

Be a team player and your teammates will help you
avoid being hit by a five-pound fluke
wielded by a pissed-off sergeant.

⌒ Parable 3: Your Guardian Angel ⌒

As the director of the Special Prosecutor's Office for Medicaid Fraud, Long Island region, I had responsibility for the office consisting of six special assistant attorneys general, nineteen auditors and twelve investigators. My job was to make sure we worked together as a team to investigate and prosecute those people who would steal funds that were designated to provide healthcare to those in need. Besides being in daily communication with both the chief auditor and chief investigator, I regularly visited the part of the office we called the "auditors' pit" to speak to the staff informally. I also visited the "bullpen" where our investigators, who were sworn police officers, conducted their business.

One such day in the summer of 1981, I wandered into the bullpen where three investigators were discussing the pre-interrogation Miranda warning named after the 1966 US Supreme Court ruling in the landmark case *Miranda v.*

Arizona. That decision (as you probably know from watching TV crime shows) required that when an individual is in custody, any statements he or she makes are inadmissible in court unless the arrestee is first warned: "You have the right to remain silent. Anything you say can and will be used against you in a court of law. You have the right to an attorney. If you cannot afford an attorney, one will be provided for you. Do you understand the rights I have just read to you?"

Two of the investigators involved in this discussion I was overhearing were former detectives with the Suffolk County Police Department. Frank Brennan was there, too, listening to the Suffolk guys extol their department's 90 percent confession rate in homicide cases, a rate far in excess of neighboring Nassau County.[2]

Another ex-Suffolk detective then joined the discussion with a story he had heard about a suspect in an armed robbery case. The robbery squad had been after this guy for weeks. While the squad had little sympathy for the victims—two drug dealers from Mastic Beach—the robber not only took money and drugs but also felt it necessary to brutally pistol-whip one of his victims. The detectives were convinced it was only a matter of time before they would have a dead drug dealer on their hands and

---

[2] This dubious distinction was corroborated by a finding of the 1989 New York State Investigation Commission report. It noted that the Suffolk County confession rate in homicide cases was "an astonishingly high figure compared to other jurisdictions, so high, in fact, that in and of itself it provokes skepticism regarding Suffolk County's use of confessions and oral admissions."

therefore would lose the case to the boys from homicide. They had arrested a guy who was sitting in their interrogation room in handcuffs. The detectives "knew" they had the right guy. His description matched the perp, and the drug dealer who avoided being beaten up had picked the suspect's picture out of a photo array of eight people.

Nevertheless, a drug dealer would not make a very sympathetic victim as far as Suffolk County jurors were concerned. A confession would put a nice red bow on the case when it was presented to the DA's office for prosecution. Unfortunately for the police, their suspect wanted to "lawyer up"—police jargon for a suspect's request for a lawyer. This request, under Miranda, would require the interrogation to stop until counsel arrived at the police station and spoke to his client. The result was preordained, as any attorney who wanted to avoid an ineffective assistance of counsel claim or a malpractice lawsuit would not let the interrogation continue. The story appeared to end at that point.

The former Suffolk detective took a breath and continued: "He didn't know his attorney's phone number, so we helped."

Although the suspect said his lawyer had an office in Suffolk County—where the robbery squad's office was located—a copy of the Manhattan phone book, which was as least three times as thick as the one that covered Suffolk County, was presented to him. The suspect's hands were still cuffed behind his back when the substantial directory was placed on the table in front of him. Before the suspect could complain about being provided the wrong phone book, a second detective picked up the book and slammed it into the back of the suspect's head, once, twice, three times, then four times.

The suspect was reeling from the sudden attack and probably suffering a slight concussion.

"Still want to call your lawyer?" a voice yelled.

The suspect immediately retracted his request for counsel and voluntarily gave the police his confession, later reduced to three written pages that the suspect voluntarily signed.

Perhaps for my benefit, the former Suffolk detective reiterated that he could not swear to the truth of the events, but that's what he *heard*.

Frank was appalled by the tactics used by the Suffolk County boys and let them know it in no uncertain terms. He was not complaining about the treatment the suspect had received, but rather by how stupid the cops were in obtaining the confession. As the conversation became more heated, three of the younger investigators gathered around.

"You probably left enough physical evidence of the beating to have even a half-assed ambulance chaser get the confession tossed out. You guys are just a bunch of ignorant gorillas," Frank said.

In response, a question was directed at Frank as to how he would have handled the situation. Instead of answering the question directly, Frank took off his tinted spectacles and told this parable of what happened in his Brooklyn homicide squad room.

After six months of investigating, Frank had finally arrested a twenty-eight-year-old who was part of a group of three whose vocation in life was to rob liquor stores at gunpoint. They worked in the Bay Ridge Sunset Park part of the borough. The trio used the same method of operation in all its stick-ups. One guy would go in first and appear to be reviewing the selection of red wine. Shortly thereafter, a second guy would enter and ask the shopkeeper about a specific brand of Scotch whisky. As the shopkeeper attended to the second customer, his back would be turned from the first. Then Customer One would draw his revolver and announce the stick up. When the shopkeeper turned to the voice, Customer Two also drew his weapon. With his hands up, the owner was hustled to the cash drawer, which he dutifully opened for four hands to scoop up the cash. To facilitate their escape, one of the thieves delivered a punch to the shopkeeper's kidney or applied a pistol butt to the base of the neck. Either treatment would result in the victim hitting the floor, where he was ordered to stay. After a quick dash out of the door and into the waiting car driven by the third accomplice, all that remained to be done was to whack up the take.

As the gang got more and more proficient, the entire job could be completed in less than three minutes.

Paulie Matti did not grow up in Brooklyn. He lived with his parents on 101st Street between First and Second Avenue in Manhattan. His parents had moved from a small town south of Florence to an Italian ghetto on the Upper East Side of New York, now called Harlem. While a few of his friends got involved in neighborhood gangs, the young Paulie spent his time at St. Lucy's Church on 104th Street as an altar boy.

By 1953, Paulie had left East Harlem, moved into the Fort Hamilton section of Brooklyn, married Enza Zecca and went to work for the US Post Office. To earn extra money for his new family, he moonlighted at Harberson Spirits on Fifth Avenue in Bay Ridge and worked from 7:00 p.m. until closing on Tuesdays, Thursdays and Fridays.

On the Thursday night in question, the two perpetrators entered the liquor store and ran the same drill. However, this time when Customer One pulled the gun, Paulie did not freeze. Instead, Paulie rushed the gunman and a struggle ensued. Paulie knocked the gunman to the floor and managed to get on top of the stunned thief, pinning his arms to the ground with his knees. Paulie called for Customer Two to help him. Customer Two did not hesitate. He ran to the two men on the floor, approached Paulie from his right side and sent a .45-caliber bullet into Paulie's brain. The force from the bullet threw Paulie off the downed perpetrator. The two robbers—now murderers—quickly fled the store. To their surprise, they were now alone as the driver of the get-away car panicked when he heard the shot and drove off, causing his cohorts to leave the scene by running down Fifth Avenue.

Pressure to catch the robbers originally rested with the robbery squad detectives, but the case was transferred to the homicide bureau the very day that Paulie's funeral mass was held at St. Lucy's. Pressure was also being exerted at the police commissioner's office by local liquor storeowners. It was the week after Thanksgiving, and with the holiday season came increased liquor sales making the stores more vulnerable targets. To appease the retailers, the commissioner took drastic action. Each of the five largest liquor stores in Brooklyn would be provided an additional "employee" from 6:00 p.m. until closing. This employee would not stock shelves, nor take inventory or wait on customers. Rather, he would sit alone on a stool in the backroom watching the sales floor. Next to him, leaning against three cases of Chianti, would be his twelve-gauge pump-action shotgun.

The odds of one of these officers catching the robbers was admittedly small, but the presence of the officers in certain high-risk areas made the shopkeepers feel safer.

Nothing happened at any of the locations until one hour before closing at Wurst's Liquor on Friday, December 11. That day had been busy, and the owners knew the cash they were about to count would add up to be one of their better days.

Approximately forty-five minutes before closing, a customer came in, followed shortly by another. They fit the descriptions given by witnesses at six other stick-ups, and that fact was not lost on Officer Warren Donovan, who quietly picked up his twelve-gauge.

The heist proceeded to play out as described by the previous victims. As Customer Two sought the shopkeeper's assistance, Customer One drew his gun and approached the intended victim from behind. Before Customer One was able to take two steps toward the store's owner, the curtain that separated the store from the stockroom parted. A blue figure shouted, "Merry Christmas," and fired a shotgun round into the store's ceiling.

As rehearsed, the store owner hit the floor, and before the perps could react, they heard the distinctive sound of a shotgun racking its next shell. Shortly thereafter, backup arrived and the two robbers were soon sitting in separate homicide squad interrogation rooms. The fact that Customer Two (henceforth, known as Perp Two) had a .45-caliber revolver when he was arrested made him the prime suspect in the Matti murder. His partner, now known as Perp One, had been armed with a .38-caliber revolver and the medical examiner confirmed Paulie's fatal wound was caused by a .45-caliber bullet. After several hours of Frank Brennan's interrogation, Perp One realized that he could be charged with Paulie's murder, even if he did not fire the killing shot.

"Felony murder is a murder committed during the commission of a felony, even if you did not fire the fatal shot, and is punishable by death in Old Sparky, the electric chair located in the death chamber at Sing Sing," Frank calmly told him and even showed him a picture of the very electric chair that was used to execute Julius and Ethel Rosenberg in 1953.

"Here's how it goes." Frank looked directly into Perp One's eyes. "You're handcuffed and shackled in your holding cell, and then you walk the last mile into the death chamber. In the center is Old Sparky. They have you sit, and they spend the next ten minutes strapping you in. Straps across your chest and arms bind you to the wooden chair. Then electrodes are placed on your ankles. Large wet sponges soaked in saltwater are placed between the metal electrodes and your ankles to ensure the electricity has as little resistance as possible. As they are doing this to you—for another ten to fifteen minutes—you get to sit and contemplate your death and think that the next time you leave that chair you will be going into a black body bag. Finally, a wet saltwater sponge is placed on your shaved head, and a metal headpiece, like a football helmet, is placed over it. A hood is then put over your face so the witnesses to the execution won't see your skin burn off your head and eyes pop out. You then get asked for any last words and you know you will now be put to a painful death. The last thing you will hear is "BANG," and two thousand volts of electricity will go through your body from your head to your feet for fifteen seconds. Your body temperature will shoot up to 140 degrees and you will fry from the inside out."

Frank could tell he was getting through to the twenty-eight-year-old man across the table.

"If you go down for robbery, you may get twenty years or less, but you will live. I know you didn't pull the trigger. Cooperate by testifying against your accomplice, and we will recommend to the district attorney to let you live. Think about it."

Frank left the room to let his words sink in. Thirty minutes later, another detective called Frank to come into the interrogation room. Perp One was ready to confess to each of the robberies and testify that his co-defendant was the triggerman. Frank told two other detectives to write down the confession in detail and have Perp One sign it, which he did.

The Suffolk County boys were singularly unimpressed with the story. "Great job, Frank," one said. "You got one dirt bag testifying against the other. Any defense attorney worth a damn will cross-examine the hell out of your witness and show he is making up the story just to avoid the death penalty."

Frank was not fazed. "Brilliant observation. One confession, a case will not make but two confessions tie it up tight. Now if you two would just keep your traps shut, I can continue.

"Perp Two was not impressed at all with the physical evidence we had against him. 'A lot of people carry .45's,' he said. He also knew that we did not have the shell casing he used to send Paulie to heaven. He had picked it up before he left the liquor store and dropped it into a sewer miles away from the store. Perp Two was also betting that any ballistic test from his .45 pistol would not be conclusive, because he was sure the bullet he fired went on a downward trajectory through Paulie's brain then into the concrete floor, rendering the resultant slug disfigured and difficult, if not impossible, to match to his gun. He also felt the same way you felt about the confession his former buddy had given.

"He said, 'I didn't shoot that clerk. The guy who did is trying to pin this on me.'

"In sum, Perp Two felt pretty confident the homicide would not stick."

Not only was the evidence thin but Perp Two was not at all impressed with Detective Brennan. He had many run-ins with the police over the years and he was convinced Brennan was a lightweight until…

Frank grabbed Perp Two by the collar of his shirt, pulled him out of the chair he was sitting in and pushed him out of interrogation room B into an eight-by-twelve-foot storeroom in the left rear corner of the precinct. The storeroom was very dark and cluttered and had obviously not been cleaned in months. Perp Two was pushed toward the six-foot-high window in the back of the room. The window looked like it had never been washed, and the accumulation of dirt and grime made the sunlight look gray. The window stood three feet off the floor, and the lower windowpane was suddenly lifted, not by Frank, but by someone dressed all in white just in Perp Two's peripheral vision.

As the figure in white lifted the window, the setting sunlight shone in, making the figure even brighter. Frank then pushed Perp Two into the opening until his head and chest were resting uncomfortably over the windowsill. It was then that Frank whispered into the ear of the prone shooter.

"You have two choices. Give me a confession, or you go out the window headfirst trying to escape."

To make his point, Frank removed the handcuffs holding Perp Two's wrists behind his back but put his knee on the small of his back.

Then the figure in white softly announced that he was Perp Two's guardian angel and casually pointed out that they were on the third story and the typical New York City story was thirteen feet. Hence, they were approximately thirty-nine feet above an alleyway that separated the precinct office from an adjoining building. The alley was twelve feet wide and was paved with concrete six inches thick, the angel explained. The angel also pointed out that although it was about 3:00 p.m. no one was to be seen in the alley because the precinct office's rear neighbor was a kosher chicken market, closed for the Sabbath. The figure continued to point out that gravity's acceleration on a falling body, thirty-three feet per second, translated to mean that Perp Two's body would hit the concrete less than one second after Frank let go, with the force of his full body weight of about 185 pounds.

"It's not the fall that kills you, it's the sudden stop on the concrete that will. If you're lucky you hit headfirst and die instantly. If you start to tumble, it will take a bit longer. Either way, remember that God is all merciful, and I will pray that God grants you mercy and you do not spend eternity in Hell."

"What's it gonna be, fella?" Frank whispered.

"You can't be serious."

As these words met Frank's ears, Frank grabbed the perp's right leg while the figure in white grabbed the left leg, and soon Perp Two was hanging face down out of the window.

"It's up to you, wise guy, or your blood will soon cover the concrete below, just like the last guy."

Looking straight down thirty-nine feet into the concrete below, Perp Two saw what looked like blood stains. There were, in fact, blood stains below the window, significant blood stains, not from prior bad guys but courtesy of the rabbi who supervised the chicken slaughterhouse next door.

"Have it your way," Brennan said.

Then the white figure said, "Our Father who art in Heaven, have mercy on the soul of…"

The prayer was quickly interrupted by the panicked voice of the figure hanging out of the window: "I did it, I shot the guy in the liquor store. Don't kill me."

Frank let Perp Two hang a few more seconds and then pulled him in. By the time his feet were planted on the storeroom's floor, the figure in white had disappeared. Frank again cuffed Perp Two and took him back to the interrogation room, where he got his full confession.

"So you see," Frank lectured the Suffolk County cops, "you can get your confession without beating up people and leaving evidence of what you did. Even if this mutt was going to change his story at trial, who would believe him that a detective and a guardian angel dressed in white hung him out of a window in order to get a confession out of him?"

"How the hell did you get an angel to pull that off?" one listener asked.

"It's easy," Frank said, "when you have a partner preparing for his retirement by going to nursing school at Bellevue."

Later that day, Frank came to my office, sat down and said, "For the record, Boss, I made the whole story up to get back at those big-mouth Suffolk detectives. Those guys are gorillas and will believe anything."

Just another parable? You decide.

LESSON LEARNED:
Use your head, not your muscle.

Rest in the Bosom of the Lord, Francis.

6
March 1976
The Trail of Blood

"Please show defense counsel People's Exhibit 3 for iden-tification," the presiding judge said.

As directed, ADA Anthony Donati handed me a clear plastic bag, about two inches square, emblazoned with the word "EVIDENCE" in red letters. The bag contained only one item: A human tooth, more accurately described as a lower left first bicuspid, or Tooth No. 21.

The owner of the tooth was Barbara Hudson, a Black woman of medium height and build, approximately 30 years of age, who was savagely raped and beaten in the bedroom of her very own apartment. The first police of-ficer to arrive on the scene was on the stand as I exam-ined the tooth, said "No objection," and returned it to the ADA. The officer then testified he found what is now Peoples Exhibit 3 under the radiator in the victim's bed-room and he subsequently determined that the victim was missing the same tooth. The officer then continued with his description of the crime scene.

He testified that the victim's bedroom was approx-imately fourteen by twelve feet and contained a closet, dressing table with a makeup mirror, two chests of drawers and a double bed. One of the two windows in the bedroom provided access to a fire escape, and that window had been forced open.

Upon further questioning by the ADA, the officer testified that while there were blood spatters on the wall by the bed and on the floor, there was surprisingly no bedding—no sheets or blankets—present, only the bare mattress, which was free of blood. He ended his testimony by saying the attack occurred in apartment 3-G of a five-story apartment building located on Middle Neck Road in Great Neck, which he described as "well-kept and occupied by middle-class tenants." As the detective's testimony in no way implicated my client, when the judge asked if I wanted to cross-examine the witness, I stood and responded, "The defense has no questions of this witness."

I knew the tide was going to rapidly turn against my client as soon as the next several prosecution witnesses testified.

I took one look at the jury, and you could see by their faces that they were shocked by the violence of this attack.

The courtrooms in the original county courthouse were cavernous. They were at least fifty feet wide and a hundred and twenty-five feet long. As Nassau grew in population, it needed more county court judges to handle more trials. That meant more courtrooms were needed as well.

To meet this need, parts of the county court moved into the West Wing, adjacent to the courthouse. The West Wing was intended to handle cases of the district court, which had jurisdiction over misdemeanors and violations. Juries in those cases were limited to six people, so the jury boxes were small by design. Even though the case against my client, the man accused of the rape and assault of Barbara Hudson, was a felony, the trial was located in one of the West Wing courtrooms. It was less than forty feet long and eighteen feet wide. In county court, the prosecution and defense tables were six feet long and placed side-by-side with ten feet between them. In district court, the counsel tables were about three feet long and were lined up one behind the other. Moreover, the room was so narrow that only five feet separated the counsel tables from the jury box. The juror in the last seat on the back row was no more than twenty-five feet away from the judge's bench and witness box.

Because our case was a felony, it required twelve jurors and two alternates. Cramming these fourteen citizens into a jury box originally designed for six people made the room all the more claustrophobic. Thus, the jurors were not only hearing the case, they were, by the sheer logistics of the room, *feeling* the case as well.

The testimony of the officer as he described the blood-shed and violence he found on the scene seemed to be underscored by the very size of the courtroom we were using for the trial.

In this case, all the prosecution had against my client was circumstantial evidence. They lacked a confession by my client, had no fingerprint evidence and only a sketchy description of the perpetrator, a Black male, approximately thirty years old, of medium height and weight, wearing a dark long-sleeved shirt and dark slacks. Thus, the circumstantial evidence that they were about to unload was the only shot they had to obtain a conviction.

My client insisted he was not guilty of the crime and

turned down a plea offer to a lesser charge with the promise of an indeterminate sentence of four to eight years. By rejecting that offer, he was on trial for rape and assault in the first degree, which carried a sentence of a minimum of twelve and a half years to a maximum of twenty-five.

ADA Anthony Donati, a seasoned and well-respected trial attorney, called his next witness, a uniformed police officer who conducted a search of the apartment building on the date of the attack. In the course of his search, this officer testified that he looked in a trash bin located below a garbage chute in the basement of the apartment house and found a yellow pillowcase, a white fitted sheet, a yellow top sheet, a white mattress cover, and a red quilt.

All of the items were stained with a reddish-brown substance he believed to be blood. All these exhibits were duly admitted into evidence, without objection. The officer also testified that the substance on the white fitted bottom sheet was still wet to the touch an hour after the attack. There was still nothing to connect my client to the crime, but the prosecution was carefully building its case brick by brick.

This fact was not lost on the jurors, who paid close attention to the testimony of each witness, waiting for the gotcha moment they knew would come—or why else would we all be there?

The jury was not disappointed as day two turned into day three. The first witness on the third day of trial was Detective Courtney Platt from the Nassau County Police Crime Scene Unit. Detective Platt was a diminutive woman, five feet, three inches, and with a thin frame. She could be seen as fragile, but her looks were deceiving. Those of us who knew her were aware that on weekends she took on the role of biker bitch, riding on the back of her husband's Indian Chieftain motorcycle with a group of police officers and ex-military bikers.

When Detective Platt arrived at the scene of the attack, she was so appalled by the violence inflicted upon Ms. Hudson, she made herself a silent promise "to get this dirtbag." At the trial, she told the jury she had been informed that bedding belonging to the victim was found in the trash bin. She took photographs of the door that led to the trash chute on the third floor. She identified a photo, and it was shown to the jury. The door was painted brown, had a handle on its left side and opened left to right. The next photo she showed to the jury was of the door, held open, and showed a chute that measured two and a half feet long and two feet wide. If a resident of the building put trash in the chute, that trash slid out of sight and ended up in a bin in the basement.

The ADA then asked the questions that I was sure were on the minds of the jurors. I knew the answer to the first question, and it would help my case, but Detective Platt's subsequent answers could lead my client into a prison cell.

Q: Were you able to isolate any fingerprints on the chute handle?

A: No. Apparently many people had touched the handle and all the fingerprints were smudged.

Q: Detective, were you able to get fingerprints from the handle on the door that gave access to the chute?

A: No prints for the same reason.

Q: Detective, did you find any other substance on the
handle?

(If a drum roll was permitted in court, the prosecutor
would have had one, but he really did not need it as the
detective responded.)

A: I found a trace amount of what I believed to be blood
on the handle.
Q: What did you do next, Detective Platt?

———

The rape took place on March 30, 1975, and DNA testing
as evidence would not make its appearance in criminal trials for some ten years in the future. Since Detective Platt
did not have such a tool available to her, what she did
next was nothing short of good old-fashioned police work.
First, she used a solution of luminol to spray the handle to
the trash chute room. She explained to the jury that luminol is a chemical that reacts with iron found in the blood's
hemoglobin and causes a chemiluminescence reaction indicated by a striking blue glow. Once she sprayed the handle and the distinctive blue glow appeared, she concluded
that blood was present on the handle. Although the trace
amount of blood was so microscopic that no other scientific tests could be conducted on the sample, the bottom
line is the investigator had found blood.

Detective Platt's next step was to spray the doorknob
to the victim's apartment inside and out. Those surfac-
es glowed blue. Heartened by her success, the Detective
sprayed each and every doorknob of the other eight apartments on the third floor. That examination indicated that

all of the doorknobs, as well as the elevator call button on the floor, tested "negative for blood." Then, assuming the perpetrator left the building using the stairway, Detective Platt sprayed the handrail going from the third floor to the second. This examination also proved negative, and the same result ensued from her examination of the second-floor landing door leading to the apartments located there. Then Detective Courtney Platt had a hunch. Maybe the perp didn't go down the stairs… maybe he went up the stairs.

Her hunch proved correct. Luminol verified blood on certain parts of the railing going up. The handle on the fourth-floor landing door was negative, but the trail reappeared on the railing again going from the fourth to the fifth floor and on the fifth-floor landing door. There were nine apartments on the fifth floor, and all nine doorknobs were sprayed looking for microscopic blood. Only one doorknob showed traces of blood, apartment 5-G.

Detective Platt's testimony was not lost on the jury. They looked like they were sitting on the edges of their seats as she explained what the prosecutor would later call "the trail of blood." That so-called trail led to my client's front door.

Once she found the blood on the doorknob, Detective Platt called for backup.

Backup came in the form of Major Crimes Squad Detective Wade Kessler. He was a fifteen-year veteran of the Nassau County Police who now became the lead detective on the case. He had spent the last six years of his career working any major crimes that occurred in the county. Kessler was six foot two and looked underfed, with a few brown hairs popping out of his nearly bald dome. In his signature bow tie, he looked more like an old-time preacher than an experienced and crafty investigator.

When he arrived on the scene, Detective Platt asked if she could accompany him to apartment 5-G. Kessler agreed to her request with one strong caveat: "Keep your mouth shut and take notes. This is my lane, and you're just a passenger."

Platt, anxious to be in on the kill, readily agreed. At about 10:00 a.m., Detective Kessler knocked on the door to apartment 5-G. A Black man, about thirty-five years old, average height and build, answered the door wearing a dark gray long-sleeved shirt and black slacks. Platt let out an audible gasp, much to the displeasure of Detective Kessler. The striking similarity to the general description of the perpetrator given by Ms. Hudson was not lost on Kessler either, but there was a lot more work to be done.

After a brief introduction, Wade Kessler advised the occupant of the apartment that they were investigating a sexual assault that occurred in the apartment house at approximately 4:00 a.m. that morning and were canvassing the building's residents, hoping someone would have information so they could catch this guy. The resident of the apartment identified himself as Reginald Smyth. He believed he had little choice but to cooperate with the police, so he invited the officers into his living room and the questioning began.

Reggie, as he was known, informed both detectives that he and his girlfriend, Kenna Braxton, had lived in the apartment for three years. She worked as a charge nurse in the intensive care unit at North Shore University

Hospital. Reggie was unemployed at the time. During the discussion with Reggie, both detectives noted two Band-Aids on his left index finger but did not make any reference to it just yet. Kessler then asked where Reggie was at 4:00 a.m. that morning, and predictably, he said he was in bed. When asked if he heard any unusual noises that morning coming from another apartment, Reggie responded he did not. Kenna Braxton came out of the bedroom. They asked her the same question. She also responded no, but volunteered that she got home from work at about 11:00 p.m. She and Reggie stayed up for a while, and then went to bed at about 1:00 a.m. She did not wake up until 9:15 a.m., and she and Reggie then had breakfast.

Kessler then asked Reggie what he did that morning. He responded by saying that he got up about 8:00 a.m., got dressed—yes, in the clothes he was currently wearing—and started making breakfast. He then went to the corner candy store to buy *The New York Times* and came back home to finish making pancake batter and preparing hash brown potatoes so they would be ready to cook when Kenna woke up. The rest of the time he spent reading the newspaper. When asked if either he or Kenna knew a Barbara Hudson, they both responded in the negative. Kessler then asked if Reggie stopped on the third floor on his way to or back from his trip to the candy store. His response struck the detective as odd.

Reggie said, "No. I try to keep myself in good shape. I do 50 pushups three times a day and always use the stairs going or coming to the apartment. I've been taking the stairs up and down every chance I get. I did this morning as well."

"All five flights of stairs?" the incredulous, non-athletic Kessler asked.

Reggie proudly responded, "Yes, sir."

It was at this time that Detective Kessler asked what happened to Reggie's left index finger. Reggie responded he was cutting potatoes for the hash browns and the knife slipped, giving him a nasty gash.

The detective then requested to see the entrance to the fire escape from Reggie's apartment. Kenna took them into the bedroom and indicated that the entrance to their fire escape was located by the second window down from the bed. When Detective Kessler opened the window, he looked down on the fire escape to the third floor. It was clearly identified by the traditional yellow police tape indicating a crime scene. Kessler reviewed in his mind the pertinent facts of the case:

1. Reggie had easy access to the victim's apartment via the fire escape in his bedroom.
2. A trail of blood led from the victim's apartment to the doorknob of his apartment.
3. There was a cut on Reggie's left index finger.
4. He matched the general description, albeit brief, of the perpetrator.

Kessler pondered whether he had probable cause to arrest. The deciding factors in his decision were the blood-splattered crime scene and the report he received of Barbara Hudson's brutal beating. Because the beating Barbara Hudson received was so vicious, Kessler felt that he could not in good conscience leave such a madman loose on the street.

"Reginald Smyth," Detective Kessler said, turning to face him, "you are under arrest for the rape of Barbara Hudson in apartment 3-G. You have the right to remain silent, the right to the presence of an attorney. If you cannot afford one, one will be appointed for you, and anything you say can be used against you in court. Do you understand that?"

Reggie just nodded his head.

"I need a verbal response."

"Yes, I understand," Reggie said.

While Kenna cried, Reggie was handcuffed and sent on his way to the Third Precinct.

Once at the police station, Reggie invoked his Miranda rights and demanded an attorney. Nevertheless, he insisted on numerous occasions that he was not guilty. With no further interrogation available, the police concentrated on collecting evidence. Reggie was fingerprinted, photographed and given a pair of hospital scrubs by a lab technician with the Scientific Investigation Bureau. He was ordered to put all his clothes in an evidence bag.

The garments included a pair of gray slacks, a dark blue long-sleeved shirt, a pair of white underpants, a short-sleeved blue undershirt and a pair of sandals. Additionally, the technician requested a blood specimen and permission to take a scraping from under his fingernails. Reggie was told he could either consent or a court order would be obtained, but his hands would have to be handcuffed behind his back until the time the court order arrived. Opting for comfort and knowing the request would be granted, he consented. This was not Reggie's first rodeo.

Detective Kessler took one of Reggie's mugshots and

created a photo array. This is an identification procedure whereby a set of six to eight photos are shown to a witness in order to identify the perpetrator of a crime. In this case, the photo array was composed of eight Black males aged thirty to forty. It was shown to Ms. Hudson, but she was unable to select any of those pictured as her assailant. Thus, without a positive ID or confession, the case had to proceed on the prosecution's trail of blood theory, the scientific examination of the evidence collected at the scene, Ms. Hudson's rape kit and the physical examination of Reginald Smyth.

———

Detective Kessler was called as the next witness. He testified to the conversation he had with Reggie on the day of his arrest and to his observation of the proximity of the Smyth apartment in relation to the Hudson apartment via the fire escape. As Kessler related what Reggie told him about his activities that morning, including his trip to get the newspaper and how he cut his finger making hash browns, you could hear a bit of sarcasm in the detective's tone, but by and large, he recited what Reggie told him accurately. On cross-examination, Kessler stated Reggie made no admissions of guilt, even when confronted with the trail of blood evidence, and to the contrary, maintained his innocence.

———

I had first met Reggie in the Nassau County Correctional Facility about two weeks after his arrest, when he was arraigned on an indictment charging him with rape in the first degree, burglary in the first degree and assault in the first degree, all of which are class B felonies and carry a maximum sentence of twenty-five years in state prison.

There was no way either he or Kenna would be able to make the $250,000 bail set by the county court judge. Additionally, Reggie had a hold from New York City for violating a probationary sentence of five years imposed upon him three years earlier. That meant even if Reggie were able to make the Nassau bail, he would be taken directly to the New York City Halls of Justice and House of Detention, affectionately known as the Tombs, located on Centre Street in downtown New York to answer for the probation violation. Opting for the more opulent and less crowded Nassau County Jail, Reggie never even considered making bail.

Early on, Reggie and I had made the decision he would not testify at the trial. That decision was predicated upon the fact that had Reggie testified, he could be cross-examined on any crime or vicious or immoral conduct he had ever committed. A recent New York Court of Appeals decision, *People v. Sandoval*, permitted the defense to file a motion to preclude the ADA from cross-examining Reggie on certain prior bad acts. But to succeed, we would have to convince the judge that if Reggie were cross-examined, there existed the potential for unfair prejudice to him that outweighed the probative value of attacking his credibility.

Our Sandoval motion was denied by the court and I tucked that decision away. I thought the judge was dead wrong, and we would be able to get a reversal on appeal if we lost the trial. In addition to the Sandoval motion, I made a *pro forma* motion to dismiss the indictment. I knew the motion would not succeed, but I had to protect the record. The only motion I wanted desperately to win was my discovery motion that would enable me to get all the results of the scientific tests that the People would attempt to place into evidence at trial. The results of those scientific tests were going to be the battlefield where we would win or lose this war. I won that motion.

———

I knew the end of day three would be when the ADA could do the most damage to our case, not from an evidentiary perspective but from strictly an emotional *tour de force*: the testimony of the victim, Ms. Barbara Hudson.

Ms. Hudson was a thirty-one-year-old assistant principal in the Smithtown school system. Although she worked in Suffolk County, Barbara loved living in Great Neck, which was just a short ride on the Long Island Railroad to New York City. She and her friends enjoyed the restaurants, plays and nightlife of the city, where she was always the life of the party. Barbara stood about five foot five and weighed 150 pounds. She wore her hair in a short Afro. She was dressed in a blue blouse and matching skirt and gave the impression of being a professional. She looked frightened but determined to go through the ordeal of testifying in court.

Ms. Hudson's testimony was brief but eloquently forceful.

The attack occurred the night before Easter Sunday. That evening, she pressed the dress she was going to wear to services, spoke to friends about their lunch plans after church and watched some TV before going to bed about 11:00 p.m. She awoke at a time she estimated was about 4:00 a.m., when she felt a hand on her right shoulder pushing her flat on the bed. As she turned, she felt the force of a fist striking her hard on her left cheek. Then she felt a series of blows raining down on her head, face, neck and stomach. Although she was dazed, she could feel her nightgown being pulled up, her panties being ripped down and the weight of the assailant penetrating her. His movements were fast and hard, pushing her body deep into the mattress. She also felt pain in her face, and felt blood going down from her mouth into her throat. She was gagging on her blood.

Ms. Hudson said that, after raping her, the assailant picked her up and threw her onto the floor. She landed on her back, and in the blue glow of her alarm clock light was able to see the assailant, a male, Black, thirty to forty years old, wearing a dark long-sleeved shirt and dark slacks. As she lay on the floor, the assailant kicked her in the stomach, causing her to double over in pain.

He then flipped her over face down and whispered, "Don't move and you will live."

Although her head was pounding and blood covered the floor, she was still able to hear her bedding being pulled from the bed and even felt part of the covers being dragged over her while she lay on the floor. Then Ms. Hudson heard the door slam closed, and the room was quiet again.

She mustered all the strength she had, turned over onto her back, struggled to get up and walked to the bathroom to obtain some towels to stop the bleeding. She turned the bedroom light on, called 911 and saw that her bed was stripped and there was "blood all over."

Ms. Hudson estimated that the entire ordeal took no more than ten to fifteen minutes, but she could not be sure. Her injuries were so severe that she needed a blood transfusion—two pints—at the hospital and stitches in her face and neck to close the most serious wounds. She ended her testimony by saying, due to the force of the punches to her face, a tooth was knocked out of her jaw.

Ms. Hudson's testimony only lasted about twenty minutes, but it was powerful, and indeed palpable, to all of us in that claustrophobic courtroom. Ms. Hudson sat ten feet away from Jurors 1 and 7 and twenty-five feet away from Jurors 6 and 12. All of the jurors were able to see the scar above Ms. Hudson's right eye and a smaller one on her left cheek when she testified or walked down the narrow walkway out of the courtroom. Having been an English major in college, Ms. Hudson was able to draw a word picture of her attack to the point we all felt we were in her bedroom that night as silent observers. The confines of the courtroom made it appear that Ms. Hudson was speaking directly to each juror as she followed the ADA's direction to look directly at the jury when she responded to his questions.

Beside me, Reggie Smyth listened carefully to her testimony, but did not react. His demeanor suggested he was hypnotized. I wondered what the jury would think about his reaction or, better put, his non-reaction to Barbara's testimony.

When ADA Donati ended his examination, the judge looked at me and asked, "Cross-examination?"

As compelling as her testimony had been, Ms. Hudson said nothing that implicated my client, so I walked over to the podium next to the jury, looked directly at her and said, "I have no questions for you, Ms. Hudson, and I wish you well in the future."

At the end of the day, outside of the courtroom, Donati accused me of grandstanding for the jury.

My response was short. "I meant every word of it."

So far, there was no testimony in the case that implicated Reggie Smyth. That would be the job of the People's last witness.

There is an unwritten rule of trial practice that states you arrange your parade of individuals to the witness stand by having your second-best witness testify first and your best witness testify last. This rule is based upon psychological studies that show people tend to remember the first (primacy) and last (recency) items in a list more acutely than the items presented in the middle. Thus, as trial counsel, you want your best witnesses in those positions.

Donati intentionally broke that rule by calling Ms. Hudson second to last. He was betting, and I believe correctly, that Ms. Hudson's testimony would be so powerful, it would be remembered no matter where he would have placed her. That left him with only one witness, Detective Lieutenant Arthur Bryant of the Scientific Investigation Bureau, to tie up all the loose ends and craft them into a jail cell for Reggie.

Bryant had over twenty years of experience working in forensic sciences and was the department's top gun. His educational achievements and reputation as a recognized leader in the field of forensics made any attempt to directly challenge his findings a long shot, even if we were able to obtain the services of another expert to do so. I was glad that's not how I decided to attack his testimony. Rather, I planned to use a concept from judo, in which a fighter tries to turn his opponent's force to his own advantage. In short, I had to make the good lieutenant *my* witness. Information I learned as a result of my granted discovery motion would be my road map to do just that.

The ADA had to prove Reggie guilty beyond a reasonable doubt; all I had to do was create doubt in the mind of one of the twelve jurors to get a hung jury. If that occurred, the DA's office might reconsider their plea offer, as opposed to re-trying the case.

After being qualified as an expert in forensic testing, Detective Bryant started his slow and methodical direct testimony by saying that the first scientific test he performed was on two sealed test tubes "containing a reddish-brown liquid." He testified that the first tube, labeled "Barbara Hudson," was tested and determined to be human blood, group O, type positive. The second tube, labeled "Reginald Smyth," also contained human blood, group B, type positive.

Bryant then proceeded to testify about the tests he conducted on the fabrics from Ms. Hudson's bedroom. He examined certain exhibits in evidence and took random samples of the dried, reddish-brown stains on the material and tested them for blood. Unfortunately, Bryant was only able to detect the blood group and not the Rh factors of positive or negative. The most significant results were as follows:

Exhibit #: Item	Samples Tested	Blood Group Results	
		Type O	Type B
23: Yellow pillowcase	10	7	3
24: White bed sheet	10	6	4
25: Yellow bed sheet	6	4	2
26: Mattress cover	5	3	2
27: Red quilt	6	3	3

Bryant continued his testimony by noting that each of the above exhibits was either torn or cut. However, he offered no opinion on how the cuts or tears were made.

With the lieutenant's testimony, Donati obtained additional circumstantial evidence that he added to the trail of blood testified to earlier in the trial by Detective Platt. His next strategic move was to follow another unwritten rule of trial practice that states, in essence, if the witness you call has testimony favorable to the defendant, it is better for the prosecution to present it to the jury as matter-of-fact evidence rather than have defense counsel jump all over it on cross-examination. Donati knew I had Bryant's full report, so he had the lieutenant state facts that were potentially helpful to my case.

1. An examination of Ms. Hudson's panties revealed four blood stains, all belonging to the O blood group. Further examination of the garment failed to reveal the presence of spermatozoa. Moreover, the rape kit evidence was also negative for sperm, indicating the perpetrator may have use a condom.
2. An examination of the clothing worn by Reggie

Smyth on the day he was arrested showed one reddish-brown stain located on the upper instep strap of his left sandal, as well as two reddish-brown stains located on the lower instep strap of his right sandal. All stains were blood group B.

One reddish-brown stain located on the lower left leg of a pair of gray slacks was from blood group B.

A minute reddish-brown stain on a pair of white underpants on the lower left seat area was also found to be blood group B.

3. An examination of several pieces of clothing seized from Reggie's clothes hamper by means of the search warrant executed on the day of his arrest included one pair of white underpants, one long-sleeved blue shirt, one short-sleeved blue shirt, a pair of gray slacks and a red and gray bathrobe.

None of those garments revealed the presence of blood.

Donati treated this testimony concerning Reggie's clothes in a nonchalant manner. That was the best he could do. While Bryant's testimony placed someone with the same blood type as Reggie at the crime scene, it did not prove it was Reggie's blood at the crime scene. His other testimony seemed consistent with the statement Reggie gave on the date of his arrest, namely, that he cut his left index finger while preparing hash browns for breakfast.

Again following the unwritten trial rule of sandwiching the best parts of your case on either side of the weakest, Donati delivered what he hoped would be his knockout punch:

Q: Detective Bryant, did you perform any other scientific tests in this case, and if so, what were they?

A: I also examined scrapings taken from under the fingernails of the defendant, Reginald Smyth, on the day he was arrested.

Q: Detective, please tell the jury the results of your examination.

A *(Looking directly at the jury, Bryant took a deep, dramatic breath and spoke slowly.)*: The scrapings on the left hand of Mr. Smyth revealed no material that could be tested. However, scrapings from the middle three fingers of his right hand revealed a reddish-brown substance that, once tested, revealed the presence of blood. As the sample was so small, I was unable to determine the blood group.

With that said, Donati told the court he had no further questions for his witness.

Now it was my turn to follow the rules of trial practice, or not. One of the chief rules is, never ask a question on cross-examination unless you know or are extremely sure of the witness's answer.

My assessment of the case at this stage was that the defense was ahead on points. Yes, there was a brutal rape. Yes, Ms. Hudson was savagely beaten. Yes, she had been a great witness. But the evidence against Reggie was all circumstantial, and I believed it to be very thin.

It is much easier to conduct a cross-examination when the evidence is stacked against you. You just come out swinging. In this case, I needed a scalpel, not a machete, as my goal was to make a few points on Detective Bryant's cross-examination and get out of Dodge. The issues of the trial would be hotly contested, but not at this point. I believed I had a good argument to counteract the People's evidence on the trail of blood. I would present that argument in my summation, but I had a cross-examination to conduct and an important witness of my own to call before we got to that point.

I first asked Detective Bryant if he had seen People's Exhibit 17 in evidence, the crime scene photos of Ms. Hudson's bedroom. He indicated he had. I asked if he knew that Ms. Hudson received two units of blood via transfusion at the hospital. He again indicated he did. I then showed the detective the photos in People's Exhibit 17 and asked:

Q: Detective, when you view the crime scene photos of Ms. Hudson's bedroom, do you observe blood on the floor by the bed and heading into the bathroom?

A: I do.

Q: Would you say there appears to be a significant amount of blood on the floor going out of the bedroom to the hallway?

A: I would.

Q: When you examined the sandals my client was wearing on the morning of his arrest, you observed and tested one blood stain on his left sandal instep strap and two stains located on his right sandal lower instep strap. Is that correct?

A: Correct.

Q: Did you carefully examine the sole of each sandal?

A: Yes.

Q: Did you observe any reddish-brown stains on the sole of either sandal?

A: No.

Q: You testified that you tested my client's underwear and found one stain on the lower left seat. Is that correct?

A: Correct.

Q: Did you diligently examine the rest of that garment, People's Exhibit 31 in evidence?

A: Yes.

Q: Did you find any other bloodstains on that garment?

A: No.

Q: Did you find one blood stain located on the lower left leg of the slacks he was wearing on the morning of his arrest?

A: Yes.

Q: Did you diligently examine the rest of that garment?

A: Yes.

Q: Did you find any other blood stains on Reggie's slacks?

A: No.

Q: What blood group did the stains on the sandals, underpants and slacks belong to?

A: Group B.

Q: What is Ms. Hudson's Blood Group?

A: Group O.

Q: What is Reginald Smyth's blood group?

A: Group B.

Q: You also testified that you examined five garments retrieved from my client's clothes hamper through the use of a search warrant. Correct?

A: Yes.

Q: Did you find any traces of blood on any of these garments?

A: No.

Q: Did you examine the cut on my client's left hand?

A: No, I did not examine it.

Q: Well, did you see it when you took your fingernail scrapings?

A: Yes.

Q: Would you agree that the cut on Reggie's left finger was less than one inch long?

A: Yes.

Q: Do you know how deep the cut on Reggie's finger was?

A: No.

Q: Would you agree that Reggie's index finger was still attached to his hand?

A: Yes.

Q: So the finger was not severed, was it?

A: The finger was not severed, correct.

That concluded my cross-examination of Detective Bryant.

ADA Donati decided he had no further questions of him, and when the detective stepped down from the witness chair, Donati announced to the court and jury: "The People rest their case."

The prosecution's case was over, and the ball was now in my court.

My plan was to call only one witness for the defense. This witness was originally reluctant to testify because she was petrified of speaking in front of a group of people. She even turned down a significant promotion at her place of employment because it required her to give presentations to various groups. When confronted with such a daunting task, the witness would start to hyperventilate, become dizzy and feel as if she was going to faint. I told the witness she needed to conquer her fear, unless she wanted to see Reggie for the next twenty years by getting on a bus and riding six hours each way to a state prison in upstate New York.

I believe fear is based, in part, upon the unknown. Two months before the trial began, I had taken the witness to the small courtroom on three separate occasions. I think those trips comforted the witness somewhat. She had expected to testify in one of the large courtrooms, as opposed to our claustrophobic one. While the walls of the small courtrooms can close in on the occupants, I think the size can also give witnesses a sense of control. On our last trip to the courtroom, we made a fortuitous discovery. The courtroom was empty, and the door was open. We went in, and I explained where the different parties would sit, especially the jury. I had her sit in the witness box while I stood at the podium from which I would conduct my examination. I also taught her a trick to remain calm. It was simple: make eye contact with *me* and talk directly to *me*, blocking out the rest of the people in the room. This is contrary to the traditional trial practice rule of having the witness look at the examiner to hear the question and then give his or her answer looking directly at the jury. I was willing to forgo eye contact with the jury if it made the witness more comfortable when she was testifying. I needed her to hold herself together, because she had the valuable testimony I needed to counter the damning evidence the People presented.

———

"The defense calls Kenna Braxton to the stand."

The court officer opened the back door of the courtroom, and in walked Kenna. The best way to describe Kenna was that she looked very much like someone we all know today but who was not born at the time of the trial. Specifically, Mr. and Mrs. Knowles's eldest daughter, Beyoncé. Kenna resembled Beyoncé both in facial and body features.

As Kenna walked down the narrow corridor between the jury box and counsel's table on the way to the witness stand, the jurors sat straight up, especially the seven men. As we had planned, Kenna wore a wine-red top and dark blue slacks that showed off her assets, without coming across as suggestive. Although she looked like a calm fashion model walking down the runway, I knew Kenna was scared to her bones.

As she was sworn in by the bailiff, I made sure the bottle of smelling salts I had brought just in case was in my front jacket pocket.

The first part of Kenna's testimony (i.e., just walking in) went as planned. The second part required Kenna to stay calm and focused during my direct examination. Under oath, Kenna told the jury that she was thirty-five years old, that she had lived with her boyfriend Reggie for the last three and a half years and that they planned to get married in the future. Kenna stated that she was a licensed registered nurse and worked at North Shore University Hospital as a charge nurse responsible for managing the care of all twenty patients in the hospital's intensive care unit.

When I felt that Kenna was getting comfortable answering the softball questions I was throwing her, I got down to the real reason she was testifying.

Q: Kenna, what time did you arrive at your apartment on March 29, 1975?

A: I arrived at our apartment 5-G at about 11:30 p.m., about a half hour after my shift at the hospital ended.

Q: Who, if anyone, was at your apartment when you got there?

A (pointing): My boyfriend, Reggie Smyth.

Q: What did you do when you got home?

A: I poured myself a glass of red wine and spoke to Reggie about the events of my day and his day before we went to bed.

Q: Did anything else occur between you and Reggie before you went to bed?

A: Yes, Reggie said he wanted to have sex.

Q: Did you respond to his request?

A: Yes, I told Reggie I didn't think it was a good idea as I just started my period that morning and I usually have a very heavy flow the first day of my cycle.

Q: Did Reggie respond?

A: Yes, Reggie said he didn't care that I was on my period and that he wanted to have sex anyway. He said he would put a towel on the bed to protect the sheets.

Q: Did you and Reggie have sexual relations that night?

A: Yes, we did.

Q: During your sexual activity, did Reggie's hand touch your vaginal area?

A: Yes.

Q: Is Reggie Smyth right- or left-handed?

A: Right-handed.

"No further questions, Judge," I said and sat down.

Donati, as I expected, was caught completely off guard. He didn't know what Kenna was going to testify about, and now the jury had an alternative answer to the blood scrapings from Reggie's right three middle fingers. I was confident he was not going to go into a frame by frame examination of Kenna's and Reggie's sexual interlude. It couldn't hurt my case if he did but would have caused embarrassment to Kenna. Donati did the one thing you should do when surprised. He asked for and got a brief recess. After collecting his thoughts, he took the approach I had expected and had prepared Kenna for.

Q: Ms. Braxton, do you know if Reggie left your bedroom during the night?

A: No, I was asleep.

Q: So, by being asleep, you cannot tell the jury if Reggie was in bed at 3:00 a.m., could you?

A: No.

Q: Nor could you tell the jury if Reggie was in bed at 4:00 a.m. or 5:00 a.m. Is that correct?

A: Correct.

"I have no further questions of Ms. Braxton, Your Honor."

After Kenna left the witness stand, I told the court, "Your Honor, the defense rests its case."

With those words, the evidentiary part of the case consisting of testimony and exhibits came to an end. All that was left were the summations by the defense and prosecution, followed by the court's charge to the jury. Television shows and movies make summations into dramatic and brilliant orations. Such orations have seldom been heard in the halls of the county court. Additionally, "summation" is a bit of a misnomer because the attorney's goal is not to summarize the facts that have been presented to the jury. Rather, the defense attorney's job is to argue the facts the jury has heard that support the position that his client is not guilty and to attack the facts the prosecution cites as evidence of guilt.

In the Smyth case, Donati and I each took more than an hour for summation. Rather than try to re-create each summation, I will just present an outline of the points counsel made.

For the Defense

There was no doubt that Ms. Hudson was an innocent victim of a crime while lying in her very own bed. There was no doubt that Ms. Hudson was savagely raped. There was no doubt that Ms. Hudson was viciously beaten.

There was, however, *substantial doubt* over who the perpetrator of this crime was.

I reminded the jury, it was the burden of the prosecution

to prove that Reginald Smyth committed these crimes beyond a reasonable doubt, and they had failed to do so.

The case against Mr. Smyth was based solely on circumstantial evidence. There was no direct evidence of his involvement in this assault—no ID, no fingerprints and no confession. There was nothing to connect him to the crime other than conjecture and supposition.

I told the jury, "When you get into the jury room, look at People's Exhibit 17, the crime scene photos placed in evidence before you. Look at all the blood on the bed and on the floor, and yet there was no blood found on the soles of Mr. Smyth's sandals and no blood found on his clothing, except for several stains consistent with a cut finger."

I asked them, "Could a cut to Mr. Smyth's index finger produce the amount of type B blood found in Ms. Hudson's bedroom?" I submitted it could not.

I predicted the prosecution would attempt to link Mr. Smyth to these crimes because his blood type is group B, but the jurors had heard that 20 percent of the African American population has that blood type.

The People wanted them to believe Mr. Smyth committed these crimes and cut his finger in the course thereof. Then he gathered the bedsheets, went to a door in the hallway that led to a trash chute and threw the evidence down the chute.

Once they believed that, the prosecution took them on a fairy tale tour of what they called the trail of blood. They said it led directly to my client's door, but when the jury examined the evidence using their own experiences, they would see that the People's theory was wrong.

The door to the trash chute opened from the left to

right. I submitted to the jury that a right-handed person holding an arm full of bed linen would hold the linen to his chest with his left hand and use his right hand to open a left-to-right door. There was no cut on Reggie's right hand.

Testing the Theory

Prior to making that statement to the jury, I had tried out my theory a number of times. In my home, we had a hallway that led to a linen closet with a door that opened from left to right. When I tried to simulate the People's position that Reggie left a bloody stain on the trash chute door with his left hand, I found out that it was more natural for a right-handed person to hold the linen to his chest with his left hand and arm and open a left-to-right door with his right hand. In the months before the trial, any friend or family member who was right-handed and came over for dinner or a drink would, at my request, take the walk down the hallway carrying whatever laundry we had in our hamper—to the utter disgust of my wife—to test how they would open the door. They always used their right hand to open the door. The same was true for opening a front door, as you will see next.

I told the jury to look at People's Exhibit 19, the photograph of Reggie's front door where the trail of blood ended. Look closely at the photograph, I told them, and they would see a doorknob and a deadbolt lock above it. I urged them again to use their experience. When a right-handed person approaches such a lock, that person puts the key in the deadbolt lock with the right hand and turns the doorknob with the left. If the person had a cut on their left index finger, I submitted that there could be a bloodstain on that doorknob.

I reminded the jury that the People also produced evidence that indicated blood was found in the fingernail scrapings of three fingers of Reggie's right hand. Kenna explained how that occurred. Her explanation made more sense than believing that only three of Reggie's ten fingers would have blood under the fingernails, given all the blood that was spattered in Ms. Hudson's bedroom.

For the Prosecution

Donati began by reminding the jury of the horrible crime that brought them all into that courtroom. On March 30, 1975, Easter Sunday, in the early morning hours, Barbara Hudson was savagely beaten, raped and left nearly unconscious. Her injuries were so severe that she needed two pints of blood in the emergency room, and a premolar, a big tooth, was knocked out of her jaw when this perpetrator punched her in the face.

How did this mad man enter Ms. Hudson's bedroom? The assailant forced open a window into her bedroom while standing on the fire escape, the fire escape that also served apartment 5-G, two stories above Ms. Hudson's.

Donati referred to the amount of blood spilled in Ms. Hudson's bedroom. He said the defense had made light of the fact that, in addition to Ms. Hudson's blood, type O, there was blood from another person—the perpetrator of this vicious crime—whose blood type was group B. Defense counsel had informed the jury that 20 percent of the African Americans in this country have group B blood type. That translated into one in five persons. And the defendant had type B blood.

Donati reminded the jury of Detective Courtney Platt's testimony. She had methodically and carefully followed a blood trail from the victim's apartment up two flights of stairs to the fifth floor and then to the only doorknob on the fifth floor that had a blood spot. That was apartment 5-G, belonging to the defendant Reginald Smyth. It was clear that the trail of blood led directly to his door.

In Donati's telling, the defense also made light of the concept of circumstantial evidence. He advised them that the judge would instruct them that the law draws no distinction between circumstantial evidence and direct evidence in terms of the weight jurors should give it.

The ADA characterized the defense's arguments as being convenient excuses, not facts.

The defense claimed Reggie cut his finger while preparing hash brown potatoes. Reggie went down to the corner store to purchase a copy of the newspaper. He walked up the stairs to his fifth-floor apartment for exercise. He had sex with his girlfriend hours before the attack.

Donati ended strong: The defense gave the jury excuses. The prosecution provided facts that pointed to only one conclusion, that Reginald Smyth was guilty.

With the summations completed, all that was left was the judge's charge to the jury on the law applicable to this case.

The Court's Charge to the Jury

The purpose of the court's charge to the jury is to give the jurors the rules they must follow in deliberation. The charge can take anywhere from an hour to several hours depending on the complexity of the case. Rather than providing the court's charge verbatim, I will hit on some of its more critical points.

In arriving at a verdict, all twelve jurors must agree. That is, all twelve jurors must agree to convict or acquit.

It is the obligation of the prosecution to prove the defendant guilty beyond a reasonable doubt.

In evaluating the evidence and the issues presented, jurors should use common sense, knowledge and experience, just as they would in making decisions in their daily lives. The judge defined "knowledge" and "experience" as the sort that an average person would acquire in life.

I had asked for this charge in our pre-charge meeting with the judge. Donati argued against it, but the judge granted my request.

The judge then defined circumstantial evidence and explained its importance. Direct evidence, he explained, is evidence of a fact based on a witness's personal knowledge or observation of that fact. A person's guilt may be proven by direct evidence if, standing alone, that evidence satisfies a jury beyond a reasonable doubt of the person's guilt of that crime.

Circumstantial evidence is inferred from direct evidence. The direct evidence is a fact that allows a juror to reasonably infer the existence or nonexistence of another fact. A person's guilt may be proved by circumstantial evidence, if that evidence, while not directly establishing guilt, gives rise to an inference of guilt beyond a reasonable doubt.

The judge provided an example: Suppose that in a trial one of the parties tried to prove that it was raining on a certain morning. A witness testified that, on that morning, she walked to the subway and as she walked, she saw rain falling, she felt it striking her face and she heard it splashing on the sidewalk. That testimony of the witness's perceptions would be direct evidence that it rained on that morning.

Suppose, on the other hand, the witness testified that the sky was clear as she walked to the subway, that she went into the subway and got on the train. While she was on the train, she saw passengers get on carrying wet umbrellas and wearing wet clothes and raincoats. The witness provided direct evidence of what she observed. And because an inference that it was raining in the area would flow naturally, reasonably and logically from that direct evidence, the witness's testimony would constitute circumstantial evidence that it was raining in the area.

The judge, as Donati had predicted in his summation, told the jury that the law draws no distinction between circumstantial evidence and direct evidence in terms of weight or importance. Either type of evidence may be enough to establish guilt beyond a reasonable doubt, depending on the facts of the case as the jury finds them to be.

Because circumstantial evidence requires the drawing of inferences, the judge explained the process involved in analyzing that evidence and what the jury had to do to return a verdict of guilty based solely on circumstantial evidence.

First, the jury must decide what facts, if any, have been proven. Any facts upon which an inference of guilt can be drawn must be proven beyond a reasonable doubt.

After jurors have determined what facts, if any, have been proven beyond a reasonable doubt, they must decide what inferences, if any, can be drawn from those facts.

Certain criteria must be met before they may draw an inference of guilt: that inference must be the only one that can fairly and reasonably be drawn from the facts; it must be consistent with the proven facts; and it must flow naturally, reasonably and logically from them.

Again, it must appear that the inference of guilt is the only one that can fairly and reasonably be drawn from the facts and that the evidence excludes to a moral certainty every reasonable hypothesis of innocence.

If there is a reasonable hypothesis from the proven facts consistent with the defendant's innocence, then the jury must find the defendant not guilty.

If the only reasonable inference the jury can find is that the defendant is guilty of a charged crime, and that inference is established beyond reasonable doubt, then they must find the defendant guilty of that crime.

Now that you, my reader, have heard the key evidence in this case and have listened to the summations and the judge's charge on the law in this case, I ask: If you were on the jury, how would you vote? Guilty or not guilty?

The jury in our case was composed of seven men and

five women between the ages of thirty and sixty. They started deliberations at noon on Tuesday. At about 3:00 p.m., we had our first request for a read-back, and it was a request for Detective Platt's testimony on the trail of blood. About two hours later, a request was made to re-hear the interview between Reggie Smith and Detective Wade Kessler. It was about six o'clock when the read-back was completed, and the judge decided to let deliberations continue another hour before sequestering the jury overnight.

Viewing the interaction among the jurors during the two read-backs, Donati and I both agreed that two middle-aged white women, Jurors 4 and 9, seemed to be leading the discussion. When no verdict was forthcoming at about 7:00 p.m., the judge ordered the jury be sequestered overnight, and they were taken to a nearby hotel.

Once the jury had filed out of the building to a waiting bus for the trip to the hotel, the two uniformed officers who had been seated in the front row of the spectator section, no more than four feet away from Reggie during the trial, asked him to stand up, handcuffed him behind his back and led him through the tunnel that connected the West Wing to the county court holding cell. From there Reggie was transported by car back to the Nassau County Jail.

The judge ordered all of us to return to the court at 9:00 a.m. for the jury to continue its deliberations.

On the second day, there was no contact from the jury all morning. Donati could not believe it was taking them so long to arrive at a verdict. Both he and Detective Kessler felt the case was a slam dunk and should have resulted in a guilty verdict the previous night. I was thinking that the longer the jurors talked about the verdict the better it was for us, and the chances of a hung jury were increased. The judge called Donati and me to his chambers at about five o'clock and was considering letting the jury deliberate to 7:00 p.m. before ordering them sequestered again for the night. The judge also commented that he was surprised that he was not informed by the jury that they were dead-locked and could not agree on the verdict.

As soon as those words left the judge's mouth, a court officer knocked on the chambers door and announced, "We have a verdict."

It took an additional twenty minutes to bring Reggie from the holding cell back into the courtroom. As he had during the entire trial, Reggie remained stoic, not saying much to me and apparently lost in his own thoughts. For me, this was the most nerve-wracking part of a trial—sitting at counsel's table, waiting for the jurors to file into the jury box and hearing those words, "Will the defendant please rise and face the jury?"

It was always my practice to stand next to my client and likewise face the jury. For the last seven days of trial, we had been together on this journey, and this was the final step.

The foreman rose to his feet and read from the verdict sheet in front of him.

"We, the jury, find the defendant, Reginald Smyth, not guilty on all counts of this indictment."

For the first time during the entire trial, Reggie showed emotion and gave me a hug. While I was in his embrace, he whispered to me, "Thank you very much for believing in me when no one else would."

Donati was completely dumbfounded; he could not be-lieve the jury arrived at a not guilty verdict when he had provided them with a mountain of evidence. Nevertheless, Donati turned around and shook my hand, congratulating me on a hard-fought trial. He then suggested I join him to ask the judge for permission to speak to any jurors who wished to do so as they were leaving the courthouse. Attorneys from both the DA's office and Legal Aid had a tradition of asking to speak to jurors after the trial in order to find out how they could have better tried their case. Many jurors were happy to have that discussion and provide their insights on the case.

By the time Donati and I got to the hallway leading out to the parking lot, only five jurors were still milling about, including the two women we thought were the leaders in the jury room. We were both congratulated on presenting our cases clearly so the facts could be understood and de-bated in the jury room. The two women jurors said they felt the circumstantial evidence was not strong enough to convict Reggie. When Donati asked why the jury disre-garded what he felt was the most damning evidence, the blood under the fingers of Reggie's right hand, Juror 9 re-sponded, "Are you two boys Italians, like me?"

We responded we were, and she proceeded to say, "You have to remember this case is about Mulignans."

I knew the term. It was a Sicilian derivation of the Italian word for eggplant and was a derogatory term used to describe Blacks.

She went on. "These people are animals, and it doesn't matter what time of the month it is. If the guy wants to have sex, he's going to have sex, and his stupid girlfriend is going to agree."

Donati and I were astounded by these comments. All the evidence presented in painstaking fashion over four days had come down to this.

From Reggie's perspective, I guess I should have replied, "Thanks for being prejudiced," but I didn't.

Epilogue

Would you have changed your verdict if you knew the reason Reggie did not testify at trial? I explained before that if he testified, he could be cross-examined on prior crimes. Reggie had a prior conviction for burglary that happened three years earlier, and for which he was serving a five-year probationary sentence. That would have been bad enough, but the facts surrounding the burglary would have also been used to cross-examine him. Remember, I lost the Sandoval motion before the trial started, and the judge said he would allow Donati to use these facts in cross-examining Reggie.

Reggie had pled guilty to the felony of burglary, in which he left his apartment by his fire escape and broke into the apartment of a couple two stories above his by forcing open a locked window. He took cash, jewelry and high-end stereo equipment. When he tried to pawn the stereo equipment, the pawn shop owner notified the police, who had alerted him to be on the lookout for the specialized equipment.

Whether Reggie committed the attack on Barbara Hudson, I don't know. He never told me he committed the crime and, on the contrary, vigorously claimed his innocence on many occasions.

When a jury brings back a verdict of not guilty, it is really saying the prosecution did not proved their case beyond a reasonable doubt. The jury does not proclaim a defendant "Innocent," just "Not Guilty." As a defense attorney, it's my job to hold the prosecution to that constitutional burden. But for Reggie's prior burglary MO, I would've felt he was not guilty of these charges.

However, I have a doubt. I just don't know if it's reasonable.

7

Circa 1972-1976

A Potpourri of Legal Nonsense

A courthouse is a village unto itself. Judges, law clerks, secretaries, court offices, court reporters (who are the biggest gossipers by far), DAs, police officers, legal aid attorneys, probation officers, social workers and, of course, the defendants comprise the cast of our very own *One Flew Over the Cuckoo's Nest*. There are so many stories that can be told about legal nonsense. These are my favorites.

Honorable Shamus O'Bragg: Nassau County Court

His Honor stood a full six feet tall. He had bright blue eyes, black-rimmed glasses, a ruddy face and stern expression. His shock of white hair glowed, especially when he dressed for court in his black robe. He *looked* like a judge. But that was as far as his legal ability went. As Robert Green Ingersoll, an American orator in the nineteenth century's Golden Age of Freethought said: "We have to remember that we have to make judges out of men and that being made to judge, their prejudices are not diminished, and their intelligence is not increased."

Judge O'Bragg was far from a legal scholar, but worse than that, he didn't really care about being a judge. He liked the work hours, the pay and being called Your Honor. His state pension was only twenty-six months away. He always looked bored while he sat on the bench and treated the attorneys who appeared before him, from both the prosecution and the defense, with disdain.

However, on this one day, the judge leapt out of his boredom and took a keen interest in a somewhat odd case. The defendant in front of him was charged with criminal possession of a dangerous weapon. According to the indictment, "the Defendant did possess a dangerous weapon with intent to use the same unlawfully against another, to wit: a crossbow."

The witness on the stand was Detective Adam Bucannon from the police department's Scientific Investigation Bureau. While Detective Bucannon was a ballistics expert, the judge ruled that he could testify as an expert on weapons in general and in this case, specifically, about a crossbow. The name of the accused, how he came into possession of the crossbow, what he was doing with it or even if he was ultimately found guilty or not are not facts many people remembered for long after the trial ended. Rather, it was the direct examination of Detective Bucannon and his interaction with Judge O'Bragg that became part of the courthouse lore.

As is the case with most disasters, ranging from malpractice to airplane crashes, there was no one single cause of the accident. Rather, it was a compilation of relatively small failures that occurred and collectively resulted in a near catastrophic event.

First, the courtroom itself played a part. Much like the district court facilities in the West Wing, this room, located in the East Wing of the Nassau County court complex, was long and narrow. It measured approximately forty feet long and twenty feet wide.

Second, the defendant had waived a jury trial, so the trier of the facts in this case was none other than the always bored and annoyed Judge O'Bragg. Thus, it was up to the judge to decide if the defendant was guilty or not. Accordingly, the conviction of the defendant hinged upon only one issue: would the judge conclude that this crossbow was readily capable of causing death or serious physical injury?

Third, the prosecutor was not prepared to question his expert effectively. While prosecutors are skilled in asking questions about pistols, revolvers and even rifles, this was the first time anyone in the courthouse was aware of a case that involved a crossbow. Accordingly, the ADA should have done his research and learned about the weapon at the center of the trial. Or, at the very least, he should have met with Detective Bucannon in advance to prepare the detective so that his testimony would clearly establish that this particular crossbow was in fact a dangerous weapon. The ADA asked poorly formed and rambling questions. The witness tried to make sense of them, but his confusion was evident. Worst of all, the judge was confused.

Approximately fifteen minutes into his rambling direct examination of Detective Bucannon, the ADA still had not gotten to that key trial issue. Instead, the ADA was all over the lot. He asked Bucannon about the history of the crossbow and the names of all the parts of the weapon. The detective droned on that the earliest crossbow appeared in Southeast Asia as early as 650 BC, and the

weapon was used in ancient Greece and Rome. He testified that even in the twentieth century, some countries'
special forces used the crossbow as an alternative to small
arms for purposes of stealth. The detective then launched
into a dissertation on the component parts of a crossbow.
The bow-like assembly is called a prod. It is mounted on a
wooden frame called a tiller. It shot an arrow-like projec-
tile called a bolt. While all this might have been useful in
a college course on ancient medieval weapons, it did little
to advance the issue at trial.

By then, Judge O'Bragg was visibly losing what precious little patience he had. Moreover, the clock in the
courtroom indicated it was 4:00 p.m. This further stressed
the judge, as he had made it his daily ritual to end the
court session promptly at 4:45, which enabled him to
leave the courthouse fifteen minutes before the rest of the
employees emptied out into the parking lot, clogging the
surrounding Mineola streets with traffic.

Cutting off Detective Bucannon mid-sentence, the
judge shouted, "Stop. All I want to know, Detective, can
this particular device discharge an arrow or bolt or whatever you call it?"

The detective turned away from the ADA, faced the
judge and spoke to him directly. "It certainly can, Your
Honor, and I will be pleased to show you."

"Then do it," the judge responded.

With that direction, the detective placed the crossbow
directly in front of the judge on his bench. He then told
the judge that to fire the weapon, one must pull back the
bowstring until it clicked on the locking mechanism.

This the judge did.

"Then, the bolt is placed on the prod and eased back onto the bowstring," Detective Bucannon instructed.

Again, the judge followed the direction.

The detective intended to say, "The weapon is now armed for firing, and all you need to do is pull the trigger."

But he never got the chance.

What exactly happened next, no one knows. All that is remembered is that, somehow, the trigger on the crossbow was pulled, sending the bolt slamming into the sheet rock at the end of the courtroom two feet to the left of a court officer, who was dozing in the spectators' seating area.

The judge was now convinced the weapon was operable.

The hole in the sheet rock remains untouched as a memorial to Judge O'Bragg. A tradition has developed in this courtroom, perpetrated by the senior court officer, who tells each new attorney assigned to Judge O'Bragg's courtroom the story of the arrow and then brings them to the hole in the wall to be rubbed for good luck.

The good luck stems from the fact that the errant arrow, fired by Judge Shamus O'Bragg did not kill or injure anyone in the courtroom.

Angus McLaren: Attorney at Law

Perhaps the most entertaining and eccentric jurist to ever grace the Nassau County District Court was the Honorable Angus McLaren. His adventures and misadventures caused some of his contemporaries to believe that Angus may have suffered from some type of mental impairment, yet no one dared to tangle with the Republican Party's good old boys' network, which had deemed it appropriate that he should wear a black robe.

The legend of Angus McLaren even preceded his days as a judge and went back to the time when he was a young attorney practicing criminal law in the county. In one particular story, Angus was asked to be second seat on the defense team in a high-profile homicide case prosecuted by ADA William "Bill" Cahn. (Cahn went on to become the district attorney of the county from 1962 to 1974.)

The key piece of evidence in the trial stood propped up on the prosecution's table, situated directly in front of the judge's bench, and the young ADA Cahn was preparing Exhibit 3 for use in the summation he was about to give the jury.

Exhibit 3 consisted of a twelve-by-eight-inch pane of glass mounted in a heavy cardboard frame. It wasn't the glass itself that was so important; rather, it was the three fingerprints on the glass, made visible by black fingerprint powder and protected with plastic strips.

Cahn intended to argue that the fingerprints on the glass window were those of the defendant who allegedly broke into a house located in the exclusive four-square-mile village of Kings Point in Great Neck. In the course of the burglary, the homeowner, a well-known criminal defense attorney in the county, and his wife came through their front door as the perpetrator tried to make his escape out of the same door.

The owners startled the burglar and vice versa. In a split second, the perpetrator fired all six rounds from his .38-caliber revolver and fled. The stolen money and jewelry would mean little to the owners who bled to death on the marble floor of their foyer.

The accused was being defended by James J. Mulholland. After graduating law school, Mulholland joined the FBI. During the Second World War, he was the resident FBI agent assigned to Long Island, and under his supervision, the bureau was able to capture the four Nazi saboteurs who landed on Amagansett on June 12, 1942, with orders to blow up key defense manufacturers on Long Island.

After the war, Mulholland stayed with the FBI for several years and then retired to start his own solo criminal defense practice in Garden City. Because he was one of Nassau's most respected defense attorneys, it was no surprise that the county court judge who was assigned to the homicide case asked Mulholland to represent the indigent fellow sitting at the defense table.

This was a high-profile case. In the late 1950s, Nassau County was the scene of only a few murders a year and had never seen a double homicide committed in the course of a home burglary. After investigating the case, Mulholland was convinced his client was not guilty of this crime, and since a conviction would put him on Sing Sing prison's death row, he accepted the assignment and put up a fierce defense for no compensation at all. Because the case on trial was a death penalty case, the court also appointed a young Angus McLaren to assist Mulholland, who would have preferred to try this case alone.

The case had advanced to the point that the attorneys were preparing their summations. That is why Exhibit 3 was on display. Mulholland knew that Cahn planned to parade it and the fingerprints he asserted belonged to the defendant in front of the jury like a flag on the Fourth of July. Mulholland wanted to take some of the sting out of this damaging evidence, so he asked to use Exhibit 3 in his summation, as well. He felt the best he could do was to hold the windowpane in front of the jury and challenge the findings that the fingerprints matched his client's. It was his contention the handprint on the glass was too large to be the handprint of his client.

Cahn jealously guarded his prize trial exhibit and refused Mulholland's request.

It ultimately took a decision by the trial judge to permit the defense's use of the exhibit during summation. The judge coupled permission with an admonition, "Just be careful with the exhibit, Mr. Mulholland."

Cahn, fit to be tied after hearing the court's decision, angrily reiterated the judge's words: "Mulholland, you be careful with my exhibit."

And true to his reputation, Mulholland was. When the appropriate time came in his summation, Mulholland walked over to the prosecution's table and carefully picked up the exhibit. After holding up the glass in front of the jury, Mulholland asked his client to show his palms to the jury and argued the handprint on the glass was too large to be his client's. Then, engaging in a maneuver that he hoped would convey to the jury neither he nor his client was running away from Exhibit 3, Mulholland walked over to the defense table and placed the exhibit gingerly in front of the accused. He returned to the podium and continued his summations and his attack on the People's case.

Because Mulholland faced the jury, his back was to both counsel tables. ADA Chan's table was set up in front of the defense table, so neither of the combatants saw Angus fiddling with the exhibit. Mulholland wasn't more than ten minutes into his passionate summation when the entire court room came to a dead stop, just milliseconds after Angus McLaren had dropped Exhibit 3 off of the counsel's table and on to the courtroom's floor, where it shattered.

Few people recall that the jury accepted Mulholland's arguments and acquitted the defendant in this case. What they do remember is that Angus McLaren dropped a key piece of evidence in a double murder case—and smashed it to pieces.

Honorable Angus McLaren: Arraignment Court Judge

Things did not improve much when Angus became the Honorable Angus McLaren. I vividly recall one Saturday morning in 1973 when I was working for Legal Aid. I was assigned to cover weekend arraignments. Unlike the city of New York, where arraignment court was held twenty-four hours a day, 365 days a year, most Nassau County arraignments were done during normal business hours, 9:00 a.m. to 4:00 p.m., Monday to Friday, with abbreviated hours on weekends. Legal Aid attorneys were on a ten-week rotation covering weekend arraignments in the county. There was no additional compensation for this task. It was just an obligation we shared. We could count on arraignment court duty to cause a disruption to weekend plans when our turn came around. To mitigate this disruption, court commenced promptly at 9:00 a.m. on Saturdays and Sundays and finished when the last case was called. Everyone in the court strove to complete the docket and get out by noon. "Get it done and get us out" was the battle cry of the day.

Learn to Listen

Before we get to Judge McLaren's classic arraignment, one that still lives in Nassau County District Court history, I would like to share my first experience doing weekend arraignments. I had been practicing law for about four weeks when I was assigned the task. As this was to be my first time flying solo, I got to the court early, at 8:00 a.m., and waited for the police officers to bring prisoners from the various precincts throughout the county to the court located in Mineola. A big part of an arraignment—the most important from the defendant's perspective—is the application to release the defendant on bail. I wanted to get background information from the individuals I would be representing so I could make a good bail pitch to the judge.

No one ever informed me about the "get it done" rule, so at about 8:45 a.m. when a court officer came into the holding cell area where I was talking to the prisoners and told me that Judge Ben Zipperman wanted to see me, I told him I needed more time to complete my interviews. As the clock approached 9:00, another officer came into the holding cell area and said, "The judge wants to see you now." I again pleaded for another fifteen minutes.

While I was speaking to my second-to-last client, the clock must have tolled nine. Two deputy sheriffs came into the holding cell area. Each of them stood over six feet tall and weighed at least 250 pounds. One sheriff called my name, and I faced him. When I did so, the other sheriff grabbed me from behind in a bear hug and picked me up off my feet. I was concerned about my paperwork, which was now falling all over the floor, so I did not realize that the first sheriff had quickly and efficiently placed handcuffs on my wrists. They then picked me up and ushered me out of the holding area to the cheers of the prisoners. I heard one say, "This is a tough county—they even arrest Legal Aid lawyers."

I found myself standing in front of Judge Zipperman, a good and kindly judge, before whom I had appeared twice before. I was still handcuffed. He started his comments by notifying me that I was in contempt of court for failing to heed his direction to come into the courtroom at 8:45 a.m. Then noting my newbie status, he gave me two rules to live by: One, when a judge tells you to come into court, you come. Two, the earlier we start on the weekends, the faster we go home, get it?

I assured His Honor, I understood completely. The judge then observed that having me in handcuffs while I represented defendants at the arraignment would, of necessity, slow down the arraignment process and hence our departure home. He ordered the handcuffs removed. Arraignment court that day started late at 9:30 a.m. and none of the court personnel were happy with the new kid.

Getting back to Judge McLaren, the purpose of an arraignment is to bring an arrested person before a neutral magistrate who will advise him of the charges made against him, his legal rights and, most importantly, determine whether the defendant will be held in jail or released on bail pending the outcome of the charges. It initially appeared that we would be going home early due to the fact that there were not that many prisoners to come before the judge. The only hang-up was that one of the thirty-six prisoners to be arraigned that morning spoke only Spanish.

When this would occur, the clerk would make a call to the court-appointed Spanish interpreter, Mirta Doyaga. To call Mirta an interpreter would not only be an understatement but an insult. I worked with interpreters before, and generally when I asked a question and the client gave a thirty-second response, the interpreter would look at me and say, "He said yes." That approach clearly did not work when trying to get the facts necessary to defend a case. Mirta did not interpret, she *translated*. I would ask a question of my client, and while I spoke, I would hear Mirta saying my words in Spanish. When the client answered in Spanish, Mirta spoke the response to me in English. Mirta was better suited to work as a simultaneous translator at the United Nations than in the Nassau County District Court. We were clearly blessed to have her, and we all enjoyed working with such a great professional. However, when the call was placed to Mirta to come to court that morning, she did not respond. Subsequent calls also went unanswered. The court clerk tried every phone number he had for Mirta, without success. The clerk also made calls to the backup interpreters, but no one could be reached. Thus, we had a real problem on our hands; no one knew what to do, especially the new kid. All we could do was wait, milling around the courtroom while the judge went into his chambers.

But then, as the horn at the fire station blew to signal the noon hour, Judge McLaren suddenly materialized in the courtroom and took his seat behind the bench. He directed the clerk to call the last case, *People v. Manny Lopez*. When the clerk tried to tell Judge McLaren that the interpreter had still not appeared, the judge gave the clerk the back of his hand and insisted that the case be called—and it was.

As Mr. Lopez was ushered into the dock to face Judge McLaren, the court clerk advised, "Mr. Lopez, you are charged with the crime of petty larceny, in that on September 15, 1972, you stole two six-packs of beer from the Westbury 7-Eleven without paying for same. How do you plead?"

Mr. Lopez looked confused and did not respond to the question posed. The silence was broken when Judge McLaren said in a loud voice, "The court will now address the defendant in his native tongue." We were all dumb-founded that the judge spoke Spanish and very happy he did. The court reporter sat straight up and poised his finger over his machine and was ready to go. Our joy was short-lived when Judge McLaren spoke the words that would go down in Nassau County history. The judge cleared his throat and in a loud booming voice and in all seriousness proceeded to ask questions.

Q: What is your name-E-O?
A: (no reply)

"No response from the defendant," the Judge noted for the record.

Q: Where do you live-E-O?
A: (no reply)

"No response from the defendant," Angus again noted for the record.

Q: Can you afford a lawyer-E-O?
A: (no reply)

"Still no response from the defendant," the judge said. "Based upon the defendant's refusal to answer my questions in this matter, his case is continued to tomorrow morning at 9:00 a.m. There being no further business before the court, the court is hereby adjourned."

With those words, Angus McLaren hurriedly left the bench and retired to his chambers, leaving the rest of us, especially Mr. Lopez, dumbfounded.

As a postscript, Mr. Lopez's case was the first one to be called Sunday morning, and the backup Spanish interpreter was present. Mirta Doyaga had been hospitalized early Saturday morning, and that was the reason no one could reach her. Perhaps as some type of consolation prize, the judge pressured the ADA to dismiss the ten-dollar shoplifting charge against Mr. Lopez because he had spent a night in jail. All in all, it worked out, and the "get it done and get us out" rule was deemed not to have been violated.

Honorable Angus McLaren: On Trial

The judge's problems with communication also followed him when he presided over a trial. The judge conducted a nonjury trial of a young Black man from Roosevelt who was charged with third-degree assault stemming from an altercation with another teen. In this particular case, the defendant was called to testify in order to refute the complainant's claim and to state that he had acted in self-defense.

Defense counsel called the defendant, Dominique Malone, as its witness, and the court clerk directed Dominique to the witness stand. The clerk told Dominique, "Remain standing and raise your right hand," which he did. The clerk continued, "Do you swear to tell the truth, the whole truth and nothing but the truth, so help you God?" to which Dominique responded he would.

In the small courtroom, the witness box was immediately adjacent to the judge's bench. If both the witness and the judge lifted their arms out from their sides, their fingertips would touch.

Dominique was clearly nervous as he sat down. He knew full well that since this was a nonjury trial, Judge McLaren would be determining whether he was guilty or not. Defense counsel had prepared Dominique to look directly at the judge when he was answering the questions and to be sincere in his response. However, as often happened in Judge McLaren's courtroom, the best laid plans of mice and men went awry.

There was no trouble during counsel's preliminary questions to his client.

Attorney: Please tell the court your name.

Witness: Dominique Malone.

Attorney: Dominique, how old are you?

Witness: Seventeen.

Attorney: Where do you live?

Witness: I live with my mom and two sisters in Roosevelt.

Attorney: Where do you go to school?

Witness: Freeport High.

Attorney: Do you know the complainant in this case, Cooper Goode?

Witness: Yeah, I have known him for about three years. We go to high school together.

Attorney: Did you see Cooper Goode on December 21, 1974, at about 10:00 p.m.?

Witness: Yeah.

Attorney: Dominique, please tell the court the circumstances under which you came into contact with Cooper Goode on that night.

Witness: I went up to Sea Cliff.

Attorney: And what did you do when you went up to Sea Cliff?

Witness: I...

Judge McLaren cut off the witness's answer.

Judge: Son, stop for a moment. Before you go any further, I would like you to tell me Cliff's last name for the record.

Witness: He ain't got no last name, Judge.

Judge: So, are you telling me you do not know Cliff's last name?

Witness: No, Judge. I told you, he don't got one. I went up to Sea Cliff.

Judge: I understand you went to see Cliff. Correct?

Witness (getting exasperated): Yes, I did.

Judge: But you don't know Cliff's last name, do you?

Witness (getting agitated): Man, I told you he don't got a last name. I just went up to Sea Cliff.

Judge (likewise getting agitated): Slow down. I know you went to see Cliff. I just want Cliff's last name. Everybody has a last name. Don't you understand?

Witness (getting more frustrated): No. No. You got it wrong. I just went to Sea Cliff.

Judge: Wrong or not, you are not leaving this witness stand until you give me Cliff's last name.

Witness (turning to his attorney): This cracker is crazy. Sea Cliff don't got no last name.

It took a very short while for this exchange to take place, and by the time the clerk of the court approached the back of the judge's chair to explain that Sea Cliff is a village located in the town of Oyster Bay in Nassau County, what had just transpired started to sink in and everyone, except the judge and the witness, was stifling laughter.

Once the judge understood where Dominique went, in typical McLaren fashion, he declared a recess.

Honorable Raymond Pendelton: County Court Judge

Judge Pendelton's stocky build, coupled with his bald crown surrounded by dark brown hair, gave him the appearance of a medieval monk with a tonsure. Monasteries were repositories of scholarship in the Middle Ages, and many of the ADAs and Legal Aid lawyers who practiced before Judge

169

Pendelton believed his chambers were a center of legal scholarship. Judge Ray, as we called him behind his back, had the legal acumen to become a judge on the New York Court of Appeals, the state's highest court, but he was content to be a county court judge presiding over felony cases.

We all wanted to appear before the judge because we knew we would learn a lot. Aside from his legal smarts, Judge Ray's baritone voice distinguished him from his colleagues. He enunciated every syllable of every word he spoke. Moreover, his vocabulary was extensive, and on occasion, we had to consult a dictionary to find the meaning of what he was saying. He was so respected that on his ascension to the New York Supreme Court, the ADAs and Legal Aid attorneys who regularly appeared before him, along with his courtroom staff, chipped in and bought him a gift, a *Webster's Unabridged Dictionary*.

More to the point, while we all wanted to try a case before Judge Pendelton, that was not possible because most of the cases in county court were resolved by a plea bargain rather than by a trial.

Shopping for a Bargain

A plea bargain is somewhat of a misnomer, as the "plea" is pretty much determined by the district attorney's office and you have to "bargain" with the judge to obtain a sentence that will keep your client out of jail or minimize the time of incarceration.

After the defendant takes a plea, plea bargains tend to come in three basic flavors in the state system:

Flavor 1: The judge agrees to sentence him to an agreed upon jail term.

Flavor 2: The judge agrees to a sentence of probation.

Flavor 3: The judge caps the sentence it imposes, say one year in jail, then makes the sentencing decision after reading the presentence report prepared by the county's department of probation, as well as hearing the position of the DA's office and arguments of defense counsel. Thus, probation is still a possibility.

There are certain legal requirements necessary to obtain the proper plea from a defendant in a criminal case. Accordingly, the judge who accepts a guilty plea follows a standard litany during which he advises the defendant of, among other things, his right to go to trial, of the right to call witnesses in his favor, that the People have to prove him guilty beyond a reasonable doubt and that the entry of a plea is the same as being found guilty after trial. When the defendant states he understands these rights and tells the court what he did to cause him to plead guilty to the charge, the plea is accepted. However, when it comes time for the pronouncement of a sentence, the judge is entitled to more latitude and can freelance his comments.

In cases where Judge Pendelton decided to pronounce a sentence of probation, he always took the opportunity to impress upon the defendant that he was getting a break and that if he came back to the judge on a violation of probation anytime in the next five years, the judge would revoke probation and send the defendant directly to prison. The judge would go into a lengthy speech on how this chance to go on probation and avoid incarceration was a gift and that gift should not be squandered. Rather, it should be cherished and taken as a turning point in the defendant's life. The judge's comments were designed to motivate a defendant to leave a life of crime while at the same time warning him of the dire consequences if he relapsed. The judge delivered these speeches as if he were a frustrated Shakespearean actor.

Every few weeks, the judge would get bored with his probation speech and spend hours crafting a new script, which he would deliver religiously and verbatim to each defendant until he once again tired of it. As a Legal Aid attorney, I found myself in Judge Pendelton's court many times in a month, so I heard the speech delivered not only to my clients, but to other defendants as well. There were times when I was in his courtroom so often, I thought I could give the probation speech myself.

On one occasion, the probation speech-of-the-month was called "The Dice of Life." Imagine these words as if they were being delivered by Richard Burton standing on a bare stage and speaking to you and only to you.

"Mr. John Lawson. May I call you John? John, you stand before me on a plea of guilty to the crime of grand larceny in the third degree, a class D felony. As you know, the maximum sentence for that felony is up to seven years incarceration in a state penitentiary.

"Did you know, John, that the word 'penitentiary' has it's roots in Medieval Latin and means a place of repentance for your transgressions? However, after reading your presentence report and the cogent sentencing memo submitted by your attorney and hearing the district attorney's office recommendation, I am not going to send you to the state penitentiary. Nor am I going to send you to the county jail.

"You, John Lawson, are the *master of your destiny.* You alone have the power to leave this courtroom by the main entrance, behind you, and emerge in liberty, or to go out the door behind me, which leads to incarceration and unfortunately, at times, despair.

"Rather than incarcerate you, John, I am going to grant you a sentence of five years probation. You have the Dice of Life in your hands now. You and you alone can roll the dice."

The judge would then make a motion like he was shaking a pair of dice in front of his body.

"You have the ability to roll the dice to freedom or to incarceration. The choice is yours and yours alone, John Lawson."

The Dice of Life speech was one of the judge's better sentencing performances. No matter how many times I heard the speech over several weeks, I never tired of it.

One day, during the sentencing of a Legal Aid client, something went awry. I was glad the client wasn't mine, so I could observe from the sidelines. This is what happened.

As Judge Pendelton got to the part of the speech where he was shaking the Dice of Life in front of the defendant, something happened that was readily apparent to all of us familiar with the speech. The judge deviated from the script. Apparently, he became annoyed by the defendant's blasé attitude and demeanor as he stood in front of him for sentencing.

Judge: Young man, do I have your unmitigated attention right now?

Defendant: Yeah.

Judge: Do you understand that what I am talking about is very serious and that your freedom is at stake? Do you understand that?

Defendant: Yes.

Judge: Do you understand that probation is a privilege, and I am giving that privilege to you? You have the power in your hands to go out this door (pointing to the main entrance to the courtroom) to freedom or to this door (pointing to the door behind the bench) back to the holding cell you just came from for months, or perhaps even years, of incarceration. Do I make myself clear as a crystal glass?

Defendant: Yes.

With that exchange over, Judge Pendelton gathered himself and went back to the script in the exact spot where he left the text, stressing that the defendant has power over his life by shaking the Dice of Life. Again, still not sure if he was getting through to the defendant or if he was comprehending what was being said, the judge continued to shake the Dice of Life in a more exaggerated and dramatic manner and said to the defendant, "Do you know what I am doing?"

The reply was not immediately forthcoming as the defendant appeared to search for the right words. Then, looking Judge Pendleton straight in the eye and with body language that indicated he got the message, the defendant loudly proclaimed, "Yes, Judge, I do. What you're saying is, if you give me probation, I shouldn't jerk you off by coming back here."

That was the last time Judge Ray used the Dice of Life speech.

8

May 1980

The One That Almost Got Away

In 1980, I worked with my colleagues to create a patient abuse hotline in the office of the Deputy Attorney General for Medicaid Fraud. The hotline was set up so that the public could report Medicaid fraud and patient abuse at nursing homes and other group homes.

On the first day the hotline was in operation, I was in my office. Senior Investigator Jack Keys showed up at my door, holding the briefcase he called his "Go Bag."

"We're riding," he said. I knew then that he had fielded the first call on the hotline.

Jack was the investigator assigned to work with me. He was a twenty-year veteran of the New York City Police Department and had become a registered nurse while still on the police force. His physical appearance would also serve us well in investigating crimes committed by an individual prone to violence. Although he only stood about five feet, seven inches tall, his broad shoulders and barrel chest showed he was a man who could handle himself. While that may not have been an asset in a Medicaid fraud case, it could not hurt to have someone like Jack beside me when I had to deal with a lowlife who used an elderly or disabled person as a personal punching bag. He also possessed an interesting personality. With his red hair and blue eyes, one moment he could look like a mischievous altar boy; in the next moment, if the situation warranted, he could turn into a pit bull whose dinner was just snatched away.

As he got behind the wheel of the office's unmarked Chevy Caprice, Jack told me that the administrator of the H. Blair Rehab and Nursing Care Center had called the hotline and said that one of her residents was assaulted by an individual believed to be an employee of the home. The elderly victim was currently at the hospital getting stitches and should be back in the home within the hour.

Blair Rehab, which was affiliated with Island University Hospital and located on its campus, had a great reputation. It always received top reviews by rating agencies, there was a good-sized waiting list for admission. "Even in the best of families …," Jack observed as we headed out. He stashed his Go Bag in the back seat.

Once at Blair, we met with its administrator, Louise Golf, who was also the current president of the County Nursing Home Administrators Association. Ms. Golf told us that the assault victim was Dorian Stillman, an eighty-year-old white male, five foot six, weighing one hundred and twenty pounds and a resident in the assisted-living part of the care center. She also explained that Mr. Stillman was ambulatory, very outgoing and a gentle soul. He had been a resident for almost nine months because he had no family to care for him after his wife passed away. He suffered from Parkinson's Disease and mild dementia.

When he heard that diagnosis, Jack hunched forward in his chair. He knew Stillman was to be the sole witness in this case, and he asked Ms. Golf about the symptoms that led to this diagnosis. The administrator responded that she had just reviewed the resident's chart and made a copy for us. Jack requested the original chart instead of a copy. We had learned from past cases that original charts could be changed, and when photocopied, the change could not be detected. In addition, I needed the original to place in evidence before the grand jury.

When Ms. Golf indicated she would be happy to give us the original chart but hospital rules required a subpoena to release the original documents, Jack immediately reached into his Go Bag and pulled out the manila folder labeled "Nassau County Grand Jury." He handed me a blank form that I proceeded to fill out and sign. Ms. Golf got her subpoena and we got the original Stillman chart, thanks to Jack.

As Jack thumbed through the patient's chart, he asked Ms. Golf if Mr. Stillman would be able to testify before the grand jury. She suggested we speak with Bethany York, the registered nurse in charge of the assisted-living unit where Mr. Stillman lived and the person most familiar with him. By this time, Mr. Stillman had returned from the hospital's emergency room, and we were told he was in his room expecting us. Room 347 was approximately thirty feet long and fourteen feet wide. It contained two beds separated by a privacy curtain. We found Mr. Stillman sitting on a recliner next to his bed. He had a bandage over his left eye that extended down the side of his face. As we entered the room, Mr. Stillman tried to stand to greet us, but we told him to stay seated. We saw a laceration on his chin that was left uncovered. Jack showed him his police shield and introduced himself as an investigator with the attorney general's office, as well as a registered nurse. He never bothered to introduce me as the attorney on the case but immediately focused on how Mr. Stillman was injured. This was not going to be a social visit.

When Jack asked what had happened, Mr. Stillman said that after lunch he went back to his room to sit in the recliner and watch TV. After a short while, an aide came into his room and told him he needed to get into bed because the aide was going home early. Stillman said he refused. The aide then grabbed him by his shoulders and shook him violently.

Mr. Stillman again refused to get in the bed. He recounted, "The man pulled me out of my chair and threw me on to the bed. Then as I tried to standup, he threw two or three fist punches at my face and then a punch into my stomach and left my room. The guy was wearing a large ring on his hand and the ring cut me. I yelled out for a corpsman. I was in the navy for thirty years and was on one of the first nuclear subs; we had the best corpsman in the entire fleet. Somebody came in to check on me and said I needed to go stateside to the hospital to get some stitches. But here I am. Ready for sea duty, sir."

As Jack's discussion continued, Mr. Stillman described the man who hit him as William, who worked as an aide and was about thirty years old. Mr. Stillman said he never liked the man because he was rough in treating him and more interested in talking to the female aides than caring for his patients.

"They want to get paid but do not want to work." That ended his recitation of the events.

We talked to Mr. Stillman's neighbor, too, but he was not of any help. He said he was asleep during the entire incident. Nevertheless, the identity of the perpetrator was already established when we spoke to the administrator, who said there was only one male aide working in the unit that afternoon. His name was William Kendall.

While we were still in Mr. Stillman's room, we had the opportunity to meet Bethany York, the nurse in charge. Bethany held a doctoral degree in nursing and was an adjunct professor at Stony Brook University Hospital. Bethany told us she took an immediate liking to "Chief," as she called Mr. Stillman, referring to his last Navy rank when he was chief of the boat, the highest non-commissioned officer on a submarine.

"I'm a navy brat," she told us. "I grew up on many bases. My dad was in the navy for thirty-five years and was an officer on a destroyer, aircraft carrier and a sub just like Chief. I grew up with sailors all my life and only made one dumb mistake… I married a Marine."

That last statement brought a smile to Stillman's swollen face.

Bethany went on. "Chief reminds me of my father, who passed away last year. I have missed my conversations with my dad, and as time went by, Chief and I have found we have a lot to talk about. Actually, Chief does most of the talking. He doesn't have any family in the state, but as my dad always said, 'Navy is family.'"

I could tell she really cared for her patient and was truly hurt that one of her own staff assaulted her friend.

When we left Mr. Stillman's room, Bethany confirmed that there was only one male aide on the floor that afternoon, William Kendall. He was a thirty-eight-year-old licensed practical nurse and had been with the facility for less than one year. Bethany told us that while Kendall was smart, he had a bad temper. Specifically, she had to counsel him as recently as two weeks ago concerning his rough treatment of another patient, and she had told him then to be more caring and compassionate of his patient's situation. Jack wanted to interview Kendall immediately. Bethany said that when she confronted Kendall about striking Mr. Stillman, he vigorously denied doing so. Nevertheless, he immediately left Blair after their discussion, hours before his shift was scheduled to end.

I asked Bethany about Mr. Stillman's mental status. She told us he had recently shown increasing signs of dementia. She advised that Mr. Stillman was able to remember events and places that took place years ago but at times had difficulty recalling what he had had for breakfast and often repeated questions, even after they had been answered. She also told us that Chief's condition varied day to day. For example, she said today he was on the top of his game when she asked him what happened, but there was no way to know what he would recall in the future.

I pointedly asked Bethany if she thought Chief could testify before the grand jury, which was sitting two days from now. She said she couldn't be sure how he would react. I asked her if she would accompany Chief to the grand jury, to which she responded, "Absolutely."

Now the ball was in my court. This was not the classic who-done-it. The identity of the perpetrator was established. I just had to prove it.

Before I left the facility, I had a brief conversation with Stillman and told him about the need to have him testify before the grand jury. I told him that Bethany would accompany him to the grand jury room, but only he and I would be able to go inside and he would tell what happened to him. Briefly, we recounted the events of his injury and his recollection was identical to what he had told Jack initially.

When I asked if he would testify for me, Stillman said he would do so as it was the right thing to do and that "there is no wrong time to do the right thing."

Two days later, Bethany escorted my main witness to the third floor of the county courthouse and met us outside of the grand jury room. When I asked Bethany, who was standing behind Mr. Stillman, how he was doing, she enthusiastically responded "fine," while vigorously shaking her head side to side.

I drew her aside so we could speak alone. She said Chief was agitated on the ride over to the courthouse, and she was not sure of what to expect. Instead of going over the facts again with Mr. Stillman, I decided to take him directly into the grand jury chamber. I told him that once the jury members arrived, the two of us would just have a conversation about how he got the cut over his eye and that some other people would be listening to us talk. He agreed and seemed upbeat as I went into the grand jury to open the case.

All grand jury rooms are configured differently. That day, we were in a room with 23 grand jurors who were sitting in a semicircle facing the witness chair. The right front of the room had a table and podium for the prosecutor. In the center was the witness chair. The court reporter sat to the left at an angle facing the witness chair. I wanted to configure the room to make it more comfortable for the witness. I asked the reporter to move to the prosecutor's desk, and I turned the witness chair forty-five degrees from the jurors and set up my chair to face the witness chair about two feet away. I wanted to make it possible for Mr. Stillman to speak directly to me and hoped to block out the rest of the people in the room.

When it was time for Stillman to be sworn in, he stood ramrod straight, raised his right hand and took the oath, responding with a definitive, "Yes, sir."

My confidence was renewed. I began asking my questions.

Q: What is your full name?

A: Dorian Stillman but everyone calls me Chief.

Q: How old are you, Chief?

A: Eighty.

Q: Where do you live?

A: Blair Rehab and Nursing Center.

Q: Were you at Blair Rehab and Nursing Center two days ago, on August 15?

A: Yes, that's where I live.

Q: What happened to your left eye, sir?

A: I think I fell down ... or someone hit me.

Q: Do you know which?

A: I don't remember.

Q: Chief, do you remember speaking with me before?

A: Yes, I do. Did we serve together on the nuclear submarine, the Robert E. Lee? You look a lot like the executive officer.

Q: No, Chief, we did not serve together. Do you remember telling me how your eye was cut?

A: I don't think we talked about it.

Q: Do you know how your eye was injured?

A: No. I just don't remember. All I recall is calling out for a corpsman to help fix my wound when I saw I was bleeding.

Q: Thanks, Chief. Let's go back outside.

Prior to the grand jury session, I had spoken with my boss, the chief of the criminal division, who agreed that we had a circumstantial evidence case against William Kendall, but unless Mr. Stillman could identify Kendall as his assailant, we would not prosecute. Clearly, Chief was not up to it. Bethany and I were disappointed by the outcome of Mr. Stillman's testimony, but Jack was clearly not accepting it. He pulled me aside and gave me an earful.

"I could arrest that guy right now on a misdemeanor assault charge. I have probable cause, but you tight-ass lawyers and your proof beyond a reasonable doubt always screw things up."

I thanked Chief Stillman and Bethany for coming, and they got up to leave. As Bethany and Chief walked down the narrow corridor that led to the elevator, Jack directed my attention to the couple. Bethany had her arm around Chief's waist, and he had his around hers. As they walked down the hallway, his hand slipped on to her rear end and gave it a squeeze.

Jack summed it all up when he said: "Once in the navy…"

Postscript

The next day, Jack and his usual partner, Frank Brennan (who you met in a previous chapter) came into my office. Jack was not wearing a suit jacket, but that was not unusual. What was unusual was the four-inch .357 Smith & Wesson on his hip. If you know anything about revolvers, a .357 Magnum is an eye-catching piece of hardware. Jack usually carried a Smith .38 Special and wore it in an ankle holster to be less conspicuous. Frank, on the other hand, usually carried his .38-caliber revolver on his hip, but this day, he came in wearing a shoulder holster that made him look like Elliot Ness. They could have worn their jackets and I would not have been the wiser as to what type of weapons they carried, but they wanted to come into my office to make a statement and a request.

"Boss, we don't like the decision you lawyers made to not prosecute a guy who puts ten stitches into an old man's head," Frank started, "but we both respect the decision you legal beagles made."

With that opening, I knew something was up.

Jack said, "Frank and I were thinking that now that your investigation is over, Mr. Kendall should be told that he will not be prosecuted for actions involving Chief Stillman and that Frank and I would like to convey the good news to him personally."

My response was that I thought it would be the right and just thing to do under the circumstances. And the investigators set out to find Mr. Kendall.

I was told they found Mr. Kendall later that day, and he spoke with Jack and Frank. I never asked, or wanted to know, what transpired in that conversation. However. I am sure these two former New York cops got Mr. Kendall's attention, and I am completely confident he got the message.

As my mama says, "It's not what you say, but *how* you say it."

⎯⁀9 ⁀⎯
October 2005

A Matter of National Security

One of the more interesting things about practicing criminal law was best described by Rick Harrison, the star of the TV show *Pawn Stars*, who says at the beginning of his show: "You never know what is going to come through that door."

Those words were never truer than on that day in early October 2005. The typical morning rush-hour traffic on the Northern State Parkway failed to materialize, and I found myself at my desk with my first cup of black coffee at a time when I was usually still sitting behind the wheel. Just as well, as my first order of business was to prepare for an Office of Professional Medical Conduct hearing in Albany ten days hence. In those years, I worked as a defense attorney representing those charged with white-collar fraud crimes, as well as physicians facing OPMC disciplinary action. You met this particular client, Dr. Daniel Ho Chang, in a previous chapter. Of course, you never get to work on one case uninterrupted for long before the phone rings with another client needing help. Around 10:00 a.m., my partner, Mike Fabisen, popped his head into my office. "We got a problem."

It turned out the problem belonged to one of Mike's

major clients, George Lincoln Shapiro. George, who preferred to be called Linc, was a real character. He was born the son of a rabbi and was proud of his Jewish heritage. However, for reasons I never discovered, he graduated from a Catholic high school, Holy Cross High School in Flushing, Queens, near the top of his class. The brothers who ran the school suggested he apply to a college in Indiana and he did. That's when Linc fell in love. Once he saw the Gold Dome, the Grotto and heard the school's "Victory March," Linc was hooked and spent the next four years obtaining a degree in civil engineering from the University of Notre Dame.

Even though he also obtained an MBA from NYU, Linc bled his alma mater's blue and gold. Every time Linc came to see Mike, you could bet he would be wearing a Notre Dame shirt or lapel pin or jacket. (We even suspected that he was wearing ND boxer shorts, but clearly could not prove it.) He was so deeply committed to his alma mater that, for the past twenty years or so, Linc and his wife, Rhonda, had season tickets to all the Notre Dame home football games. Sometimes they flew from La Guardia Airport to South Bend; other times they drove their kelly green RAV4 from their Suffolk County home to the game. Linc and Rhonda loved being on campus.

To sum up how Linc felt about Notre Dame football, he would often quote Coach Lou Holtz, who led Notre Dame from '86 to '96, saying, "God doesn't care who wins football games, but his mother does."

Linc was also active in the school's alumni association and interviewed applicants to the school who lived in the New York City area. Despite being a Notre Dame Catholic,

Linc did not leave his Jewish roots behind and was heavily involved in raising money for the United Jewish Appeal and his synagogue.

It seemed that two FBI agents had come to Linc's Long Island office and wanted to speak to him, but they refused to tell his secretary the purpose of the visit. This concerned Linc, and he called Mike. As I had expertise in dealing with the FBI, Mike wanted me to contact Linc right away. This appeared to be an issue that I could quickly resolve, which was a good thing, because I wanted to get back to Dr. Chang's prep.

When I called Linc on his private number, I asked that the call be transferred to his secretary so that I could speak to the agents. When one of them came on the line, I introduced myself as Linc's lawyer and found out I was speaking to Special Agent Jason Grattan. I assured Agent Grattan that Linc and I would be happy to schedule an interview with him early the next week.

That's when Grattan immediately cut me off. "This interview has to be done now. This is a Matter of National Security."

I told the agent that I was not going to commit legal malpractice or lose my license by having my client speak to law enforcement before I had a chance to meet with him and know the issues to be discussed.

My concerns meant absolutely nothing to Agent Grattan, who reiterated, this time in a hushed tone, "This is a Matter of National Security."

When I inquired specifically what the Matter of National Security was, the agent predictably declined to discuss it on the phone.

This conversation was going nowhere fast. I certainly did not want Linc talking to the agents without a lawyer, especially since Agent Grattan was being so cryptic, but I knew it wasn't good to be seen as uncooperative in a Matter of National Security. While I weighed this bad thing against that bad thing, Grattan dropped the C-word.

"*Counselor*," he said in a condescending tone, "what don't you understand about a Matter of National Security?"

In the New York courts where I grew up, when a judge or an adversary called you "counselor," they really meant "shithead." I was quickly getting pissed but having a fight over something that we knew nothing about was counter to Linc's interests.

It was then I proposed a compromise. Could we meet in twenty-four hours at my office? Actually, the Feds had very little choice if they wanted to talk to Linc. They were going to either accept my terms or they would not speak to him. The agent understood this very well and agreed to meet with us the next day, Wednesday, at 9:00 a.m. at my office. After disconnecting from Agent Grattan, I told Linc to cancel his plans for the rest of the day, and to get down to my office ASAP.

Two hours later, Linc stood at my office door. He stood at about five feet, ten inches and weighed approximately 170 pounds. He was bald except for a fringe of gray hair. His only other distinctive feature was a thick gray mustache that went from the bottom of his nose to the top of his lip and then from one corner of his mouth to the other.[3]

---

[3] Charles Dickens wrote in *A Christmas Carol*: "This must be distinctly understood, or nothing wonderful can come of the story I'm about to relate."

After the usual hellos, I told Linc that we had to discuss some ground rules. Because we did not have a lot of time for preparation and he was being charged my standard hourly rate, it would be in his enlightened self-interest to tell me the truth, the whole truth and nothing but the truth. Because I needed Linc to be completely honest with me, I related a story about two physicians who were being investigated by OPMC. They were accused of providing physical medicine treatments to patients who did not need rehab services. They got my "tell me the truth" speech and we spent the next three hours going over various printouts from EMG (an electromyograph, also known as nerve conduction) test reports, which supported the treatments they performed and billed. It was around 8:00 p.m. when the meeting ended, and my partner Alex and I headed for the elevators fifteen minutes later. We were both surprised to see the two physicians still by the elevator bank on our floor.

When we asked if they were OK, the junior physician, without apologizing, said, "We lied to you. We faked the EMG reports."

Then, the four of us went back to the conference room and spent the next two hours getting the truth out.

I then asked Linc the $64,000 questions. "Do you now work for or have you ever worked as an agent of a foreign government? Are you involved in any way with an activity that would cause damage to the interests of the United States government or its citizens?"

I got the expected replies and followed up with, "Do you have any knowledge of anyone or anything that could cause damage to the United States or its citizens?"

This time the reply was a more emphatic no. A few more similar questions followed until I was reasonably sure that Linc was being truthful.

Our next decision was whether to speak to the FBI agents the next morning or decline to do so. I told Linc that, in my opinion, if the investigation really pertained to a Matter of National Security and we refused the meeting, the Feds' next move would be to issue a subpoena for him to testify before a federal grand jury. In the grand jury, Linc would be alone, as a witness is not entitled to have an attorney with him in a federal grand jury chamber.

After considering our options, Linc felt it would be better to have me with him in the initial FBI interview.

I then changed the subject from the legal issues to personal background questions in order to get a better feel for the person I was representing. When I asked Linc exactly what he did for a living, he answered by telling me a story.

His grandmother and grandfather came to this country from Poland in 1913 and shortly thereafter purchased property twenty miles east of New York City in Queens County. His grandfather started building single-family homes on the property. When his grandfather died in the 1918 Spanish flu pandemic, his grandmother and father took over the business. Linc's dad continued to build single-family homes, expanding into Brooklyn and later began developing larger apartment complexes. The Shapiro Organization grew out of the single-family-home business and concentrated exclusively on constructing and managing high-end apartment complexes and class A office buildings throughout Manhattan, Queens and

Long Island. Linc oversaw the business and five large office complexes. On a day-to-day basis, the business was run by his eldest, Christine, and her two brothers, Ronald and Michael. The company was looking to merge with or acquire several out-of-state real estate entities to double Shapiro's holdings.

When I asked Linc which properties he was personally involved with, he listed five office buildings. I then asked him to get me a list of all tenants in those five properties and a list of who his main contacts were at each property. Even though we had no idea what the FBI wanted with us, I wanted to be as prepared as possible.

We then considered any foreign nationals that Linc may have known either in his business or in his philanthropic activities. I centered the discussion on individuals from Russia, North Korea, China and Israel. Linc stated he had no personal contact with citizens from these countries, except for several prominent Israelis he met during his United Jewish Appeal activities, including some high-ranking military officers. However, none of these individuals ever asked him any questions to do with anything that could be considered national security.

As Linc put it, "If the Mossad was reaching out to me, the state of Israel is doomed."

I also gave Linc a list of homework assignments to help us prepare as much as possible for the meeting that was then only about eleven hours away.

Linc arrived at my office promptly at 7:30 a.m. the next day and brought his completed homework, consisting of a list of each property owned or managed by the Shapiro Organization, the tenants in each building and a printout of all telephone calls made on Linc's office, cell and home phones for the last four weeks. All that was left to do was to keep Linc calm and explain to him how I thought the meeting would proceed and how we would respond to the FBI's questions.

I then showed Linc the room we would use for the interview. It was one of our interior conference rooms with a table six feet long and about three feet wide. Linc and I would sit on one side of the table with our backs to the glass wall separating the room from the corridor. The federal agents would be on the other side, looking out. I wanted our guests to know that at any time anyone could walk down the corridor and observe their demeanor. Linc would wait in my office until the agents were seated, and then I would bring him in and sit him diagonally across from the lead investigator.

I emphasized three pieces of instruction to Linc:

First, tell the truth. Lying to an FBI Agent can constitute obstruction of justice, a federal felony. If for any reason, he felt he could not tell the truth, he should ask for a break to speak with me.

Second, he needed to listen to the questions he was asked. If he needed clarification, he should ask before he tried to answer. Then, he should answer the question narrowly, with no elaboration.

Third, remember "the sign." I couldn't tell him to shut up since we were cooperating with law enforcement, nor could I kick him under the table. (I did that once in a hearing in Columbus, Ohio, and the client jumped out of his chair to the amusement of the hearing panel.) If Linc talked too much or ventured into dangerous territory, I would give him our agreed-upon sign. I would keep my coffee mug in a position away from him, but if I moved the mug and placed it between us, he should take stock of how he was answering the question and react calmly so as not to give away the signal.

We then reviewed our game plan. We would start the interview, and once we got a fairly good idea where all this was heading, I would call for a break to discuss the situation with Linc. I was still hoping that this interview was about a background check the bureau was conducting, but my gut told me we were in for a fight.

Lastly, I reiterated the first and most important rule: tell the truth.

As the clock struck nine, I got a call from our receptionist. "Two FBI agents are here to see you."

I met the two agents in the lobby. The lead agent was the man I had spoken to on the phone, Special Agent Jason Grattan. He was at least six feet tall and appeared to weigh 250 pounds of muscle. He reminded me of the former New England Patriot linebacker Tedy Bruschi but without Tedy's signature smile. He wore what appeared to be an expensive dark blue three-piece suit, a neatly starched white shirt with French cuffs held together by FBI seal cufflinks and a red tie. Agent Grattan then introduced his partner, Special Agent Lara Martin, who wore a conservative black business suit that accented her shoulder-length blond hair. Tall and thin, she looked more like a fashion model than a gun-toting cop.

In order to extract a modicum of revenge for Grattan's "Counselor" remark and to let my guests know this was not my first FBI rodeo, I asked to see their credentials.

While FBI agents do carry small badges, the proper way to identify an agent is through their credentials, consisting of a leather wallet that holds two cards, one indicating FBI, the other the agent's photo and signature. Most people wouldn't know to ask for the full spread. I wanted them to know I wasn't one of those people.

I escorted Agents Grattan and Martin to the conference room and offered coffee.

Instead of politely refusing the offer, Agent Grattan said brusquely, "No. Where is Mr. Shapiro? You have already delayed this meeting long enough." (You can clearly see this was going to be a fun way to spend a Wednesday morning.)

I left the conference room, took my sweet time and returned with Linc. Both agents stood and introduced themselves. I introduced my client as "Linc," but Agent Grattan opted for the more formal "Mr. Shapiro."

As soon as we were all seated, Grattan delivered a speech that it was the bureau's mission to protect the security of the United States and its citizens. He and Agent Martin were assigned to the bureau's counter-intelligence unit, and their mission was to "identify and neutralize ongoing security threats from foreign intelligence services." He then appealed to Mr. Shapiro's sense of patriotism and said he was critical to an active investigation the bureau was conducting. Grattan made it very clear, on at least two separate occasions, that the FBI was not investigating Mr. Shapiro or his companies. The FBI wanted his full and complete cooperation on a Matter of National Security. Grattan concluded by saying he could not give us more information about the FBI inquiry because it was strictly confidential but reiterated that national security was at risk.

Linc said he was happy to cooperate with the investigation as America "helped my family build a large and successful business from the $100 my grandparents brought with them from the old country."

I was intrigued. What could Linc possibly know about espionage that affected national security? All we could do was wait for the bureau's next move, which came from Agent Martin.

"Before we begin," she said, "Mr. Shapiro, could you please verify some personal information for us?"

Agent Martin then proceeded to verify Mr. Shapiro's full name, including nickname, Linc; home address; date of birth; and Social Security number. She also confirmed that his main office was located on Route 110 in Melville, that he was married to Rhonda and that they have three children, Christine, Ronald and Michael. Their home was located in Nissequogue, Suffolk County, and Linc drove a red Range Rover with the license plate number "Shapiro 1."

While I was sure that some of this information was required for the FBI's 302 report (a form designed to record a witness interview), I also believed it was more of a "we know where you live" tactic. It was a way of letting Linc know the FBI already knew a lot about him, so he should not try to lie.

Agent Grattan then took over. For the third time, he said, "Mr. Shapiro, you are not a subject of this investigation. Rather, we want your cooperation on a Matter of National Security."

I was going to interject at this point and tell Agent

Grattan that we understood what he was after and perhaps we should just get to the matter at hand. As I was about to do so, Agent Grattan got to the heart of the issue.

"Mr. Shapiro, we know you were in New York City on Monday. We know you parked your Range Rover at the Barrow Street garage. Sir, am I correct so far?

"Yes."

Grattan continued. "At about 4:35 that afternoon, you walked down Seventh Avenue heading south towards Barrow Street. You were on the east side of the street. Halfway down Seventh Avenue, a green 1992 Oldsmobile Cutlass was parked on the same side of the street as you. You approached the driver's side window, and the window behind him opened. You had a thirty-five- to forty-five-second discussion with the person in the rear seat. We want to know, who was in the car? What did the two of you discuss? What was in the manila envelope he gave you?"

It was easy to see the shock on Linc's face, and he was only able to get out one sentence: "That never happened."

Agent Grattan said, "Yes it did, Mr. Shapiro, and you and I both know it. I'm asking for your help. Will you give it to me?"

This time, Linc's response was more forceful. "What you said never occurred. While I was walking down Seventh Avenue on the way to the garage, I spoke to no one. Not by a car, a bus or a train. No one."

The denial was immediately met with an equally insistent retort. "Fine, Mr. Shapiro, we will do it the hard way. What were you doing in New York City on Monday?"

My rule during an interview, or in this case an interrogation, was not to allow a client to answer a question unless I was reasonably sure how he or she would respond. We just found out what the FBI wanted, and we had no prior idea that the subject of the inquiry would be about a specific incident on a specific day. We had spent yesterday's prep time doing a macro review of Linc's business dealings, but the real issue was about an alleged one-minute conversation on a busy New York street. Before I would let Linc answer any more questions—and no doubt, to further ingratiate myself to the FBI—I told the agents the interview had to stop while I spoke to my client.

Agent Grattan had no choice if he wanted another shot at getting Mr. Shapiro to cooperate. He could agree to us taking a break, or he could get up and leave. Candidly, I didn't care if he stayed or not. The break that ensued lasted for about an hour.

During our private discussion, Linc was clearly upset by Agent Grattan's questioning. However, it was not the clandestine street meeting involving national security that caused him angst, fear and embarrassment. Those reactions came from the other events of that day, which I would soon learn from Linc.

We discussed ending the agents' questioning then and there. The knowledge that Grattan either had or easily could obtain a subpoena requiring Linc to testify before a grand jury was the deciding factor. If Linc had to go to the grand jury, he would have to bear his soul to sixteen to twenty-three strangers and an assistant United States attorney. He would also have a sworn transcript of the events on the record.

While I could not assure Linc that we could avoid an embarrassing grand jury appearance even if he answered the agents' questions, I thought it was worth a shot. And besides, we had the truth on our side. Linc swore up and down that the meeting described by Grattan "never, ever happened."

No matter how I pressed him about the alleged meeting, he denied it. I reminded Linc that because of our attorney-client privilege, I could not discuss with anyone what he told me. Linc understood, and still he maintained the meet never occurred.

I also reminded Linc that he had to convince the agents he was telling the truth and was sincerely cooperating. In order to do that, I would have to let the government take their best shot at him, and he would have to answer the agents' questions without me barging in. In short, we did not want to give the impression that I was controlling or coaching him.

I then repeated my mantra to Linc: listen to the question, understand the question and answer just the question. I also reminded him not to forget the coffee mug sign I would give if he was talking too much or getting off topic.

When I asked if Linc was prepared to go forward, he said, "From my perspective, we are playing defense. The other team has the ball on our one-yard line, and it's fourth down. We will stand our ground and defend the goal line because we are in the right, and the right always prevails."

With that mindset, we returned to the fray.

When we got back to the conference room, Grattan was not happy about waiting so long. "Are we ready to proceed?" he asked curtly as we sat down. Linc nodded in the affirmative.

Q: My last question was, what were you doing in New York City this past Monday?

A: Having lunch with my friends.

Q: What time did you meet your friends?

A: About 12:45.

Q: What are the names of the friends you had lunch with?

As Linc answered the question, Agent Martin took down the names of the three men and asked Linc to spell their last names.

Q: Where did you and your three friends have lunch?

A: The Stonewall Inn at 53 Christopher Street.

As soon as Linc said the Stonewall Inn, the agents looked at each other.[4] They seemed to know at once about the Stonewall.

Q: How long were you at the Stonewall Inn?

A: About an hour and a half.

Q: Where did you go then?

A: The Melissa Joy Club on Grove Street, between Seventh Avenue and Waverly Place.

Q: What is the Melissa Joy Club?

A: It's a members-only club where you can go to relax and meet other members.

---

[4] The Stonewall Inn is a gay bar and tavern in New York's Greenwich Village and was the scene of the 1969 Stonewall riots between the city police and the inn's gay and lesbian patrons that ultimately resulted in New York City's first Gay Pride Parade. Today, the Stonewall Inn is a national historical monument dedicated to the LGBTQ civil rights movement.

Q: How long have you been a member?

A: Six years.

Q: What time did you leave the club?

A: About 4:30.

Q: Where did you go next?

A: To get my car at the Barrow Street garage.

Q: How did you get to the Barrow Street garage?

A: I walked down Grove Street to Seventh Avenue and went south on Seventh and turned west onto Barrow.

Q: As you walked south on Seventh, which side of the street were you on?

A: The east side of Seventh.

Q: Then?

A: I took Barrow Street to the garage.

Q: So at least we agree you were on Seventh Avenue about 4:30 pm on Monday. Is that correct?

A: Correct.

Q: Did anyone in your office know you were down in Greenwich Village on Monday afternoon?

A: No.

Q: Did anyone in your family know you were in Greenwich Village on Monday afternoon?

A: No.

Q: Did you speak to anyone seated in a parked car on Seventh Avenue approximately halfway between Grove Street and Barrow?

A: No. Definitely not. No.

That response did not sit well with Agent Grattan. He pushed his chair straight back into the wall, stood up, removed his suit jacket and said, "George, (now not Mr.

Shapiro) I don't believe you."

When the agent ripped off his suit jacket, he revealed the 9mm SIG Sauer pistol hanging off his left shoulder with two ammo clips in a magazine holder under his right.

That was when the threats, which I told Agent Grattan I did not appreciate, started.

"George, I originally thought of you as a witness. Now I can't be sure you're not a part of a conspiracy to damage the national security of the United States. We will now have to interview the guys you had lunch with. And I will also have to speak to your wife and children and maybe some of your co-workers about this entire matter."

Linc's denials got more and more emphatic, to the point of frustrating Grattan so much that he stepped out of character as a federal agent.

"Cut the shit, George." After a pause, when the agent could be seen debating whether to say his next sentence or not, he continued. "We had you under surveillance, and we have photos. Come clean now, and I will not arrest you for obstructing justice for lying to the FBI, and you will not spend the next five years in a six-by-eight-foot cell."

Before I had a chance to react to that bombshell, Linc stood up and said in a loud clear voice, "You're the one full of shit. You have no photos because what you say never happened."

As voices started to escalate, it was time to stop the interview. I asked the agents to speak with me in my office.

We were not happy with each other. The agents thought Linc was lying and said so. I told them they were bullying Linc, and I did not appreciate the apparent threat to out him to his family and friends if he did not say what

they wanted to hear. As our conversation got more heated, I suggested a fifteen-minute break for us to regroup.
The agents agreed.

When we reconvened, I asked the obvious question to
the agents. If they were so sure that Linc was the subject
of their case, the one way to solve the issue was to show us
the photos and establish once and for all who was telling
the truth.

Grattan predictably responded, "You can't see the pictures. It's a Matter of National Security."

Of course it was.

I responded, "I can't, but you certainly can."

As I said those words, I saw Agent Martin look at her
senior colleague with a facial expression that seemed to
say, "I never looked at the photos." Agent Grattan must
have noted her expression but sat stone-faced as if he
were playing poker and wanted to convince me he had a
winning hand. In the short time that I worked with Linc, I
had come to believe he was telling me the truth. I was totally convinced he did not stop at the car, and that meant
that Agent Grattan was bluffing. It was now time to call
the bluff and go all in with our chips. I reiterated my request that the agents look at the pictures.

Grattan again did not respond.

As we were clearly going nowhere at the speed of
sound, I suggested we reconvene the next morning at nine
o'clock. That would give the agents a chance to re-ex-
amine their evidence in light of our complete denials and
also give me a chance to confer with Linc again now that
I knew what we were talking about. I told the agents it
wouldn't be the first time a client changed his story after

being confronted with evidence and the charge of obstructing justice. The agents reluctantly agreed. Before the agents left at 12:30, I asked them to consider the fact that Linc had just disclosed very personal information about his sexual orientation to them, information his family, friends and business associates were unaware of. If he was going to lie, Linc would not have disclosed such sensitive information concerning his life.

I think Agent Martin understood what I was saying. Agent Grattan did not care.

The timing of the agents' departure worked out well from my perspective. I had my paralegal, Linda, ready to drive Linc to Elmont, a short distance away from the office, for a 1:30 appointment. In the interim, I needed Linc to calm down and rest some.

What was in Elmont? Well, it wasn't really a "what." It was a "who," a friend of mine, Jerry Spillane. I first met Jerry some twenty-five years earlier, while he was finishing his criminal justice degree at John Jay College in New York City. Jerry joined the Nassau County Police Department and was assigned to the scientific investigation bureau. When he retired from the department, Captain Jerry Spillane was a noted polygrapher with a statewide and national reputation. He had attended the FBI Academy for law enforcement officers at Quantico, Virginia, as well as the FBI's polygrapher training course. He served as a director of the American Polygraph Association.

During our hourlong break from the interview, I had rung Jerry to call in a favor. If I was going to use a polygraph test to defend Linc against the FBI's allegations, I needed a polygrapher the bureau would respect.

I wanted the polygraph test to be conducted at Jerry's office due to its unique set up. His office suite had one room designed to resemble a dimly lit interrogation room of the sort often used as a set on TV shows. A fake two-way mirror hung on one wall. The stark metal table and two metal chairs were designed to make a subject feel uncomfortable, which is also what people felt when they first met Jerry in his office. He was not a tall man. He was wide, but clearly from muscle instead of fat. He had huge hands, and when he greeted you with a handshake, your hand was enveloped in his. I knew Jerry was a fun-loving guy full of quips and jabs, mostly directed at the attorneys who hired him, but when working, Jerry was all business, somber as an undertaker and tough as a boxer. Jerry's services involved more than just operating the polygraph; he was also an ace interrogator. Jerry's MO was to speak to the client about the facts of the case, dissect the client's version of the facts, challenge his statements and then conduct the polygraph test. On several occasions, after spending two to three hours with a client, Jerry would call me and tell me he didn't perform the polygraph test because the client admitted he did it—even before being told, "The polygraph knows all."

As usual, I faxed the retention letter to Jerry so as to hire him under my attorney-client privilege in representing Linc.

When my paralegal and Linc left for Jerry's office, I took a brief lunch break. I felt drained and could only imagine how Linc felt. He was accused of participating in a serious felony he did not commit. Moreover, there was the distinct possibility that the fact he had been leading a secret double life was about to be revealed. I was sure he pondered how that revelation would impact his marriage, children, business and his work at his beloved Notre Dame. He might well feel that there was no way out of the dilemma he faced.

At least not yet.

I want to be clear about what I expected from Spillane. I sent Linc for a polygraph test, not a lie-detector test. There is more belief in the existence of Santa Claus than in the machine that can detect lies. Indeed, polygraph tests have been rejected as evidence in court because they have been deemed unreliable. Notwithstanding that finding, the polygraph is used by industry and government agencies, including the FBI, Drug Enforcement Administration and even the Central Intelligence Agency, to spot deceptive conduct.

The next day, I planned to ask Agent Grattan to schedule a polygraph test for Linc. Before I made that offer, I had to see in advance how Linc would do. Spillane's polygraph would give me that answer.

What would Spillane's test be like? Simply put, the test that would cost Linc $650 would measure certain physiological responses. The test would consist of a pneumograph that would be wrapped around the subject's chest to measure the depth and frequency of respiration, a blood-pressure cuff to measure pressure and heart rate and an electrode placed on two of the subject's fingers to measure electrodermal response. Lastly, a sensor would be placed under a cushion of the subject's chair to detect movement.

The next phase would be the test itself. The examiner would create three different types of questions to ask during the test: control questions, relevant questions and irrelevant questions. In this case, the questions asked could be:

What is your date of birth? (*Control*)

Did you ever betray the United States government? (*Relevant*)

Did you meet an individual in a green car located on Seventh Avenue on Monday? (*Relevant*)

Is today Thursday? (*Irrelevant*)

The test usually consists of ten to fifteen questions repeated three to six times and can take anywhere from two to three hours to complete. When concluded, the examiner reviews the charts and notes the subject's physical reaction to the question asked, to the answer given and to the same question previously asked. Based upon experience, a trained polygrapher can conclude that the subject's responses were deceptive or truthful or that the test was deemed inconclusive.

I waited anxiously for Jerry's call, and when it came in, Jerry's professional opinion was that Linc "was being truthful when he denied having a conversation with the unknown person in the parked vehicle."

I told Linc to go home and get a good night's sleep, because I felt we were now in a great position to fight the allegations made against him. Even with that good news, Linc spent the entire night tossing and turning, more worried about the damage the revelations would cause him from a family perspective than from any criminal charges.

At 9:00 a.m. sharp, I was advised that the agents were in the lobby. "Here we go again," I said to Linc as he assumed his chair in the same conference room we used the day before.

However, when I greeted the agents, I felt the dynamic had changed. Agent Grattan still wore his bureau cufflinks, but this time held a Starbucks coffee cup. Instead of his dark blue three-piece suit, he wore a blue blazer and khaki slacks. Agent Martin also appeared more casual, with her blond hair in a ponytail and wearing a skirt and blouse with a matching blazer. I knew Linc would love her outfit. The blazer was kelly green. As we went to the conference room where Linc was already seated, I thought this was going to be a Good Cop Thursday, instead of yesterday's Bad Cop Wednesday.

Overnight, I had changed my strategy and wanted to take the offense to start this quarter. I planned to share the polygraph results obtained by Spillane and then offer Linc to the bureau for a polygraph test at their Long Island office just up Route 110 from the Shapiro Organization.

Before I got a chance to introduce the subject, and even before Grattan sat down, he said, "George, can Lara (He said Lara, not Agent Martin. Something was up.) ask you a few questions before we start?"

Before I could respond, Linc said, "Of course."

His agreement meant that I would now have to use the Spillane report to counter the questions I expected the agent to ask.

Agent Martin took a seat at the head of the table, right next to Linc. She then began asking her questions:

Q: George, do you own a toupee?
A: No, I do not.
Q: Have you ever worn a toupee?

A: No.

Q: Have you ever worn a wig?

Linc thought for a moment and then smiled.

A: Yes, I have. Two years ago, my synagogue had a service to celebrate the festival of Purim, which recalls the deliverance of the Jews from imminent destruction at the hands of the Persians. As told in the Book of Esther, at the start of the story we call the Megillah, she conceals her identity. In memory of that story, people usually come to the festival in costume. Two years ago, I dressed as Moses and wore a long shoulder-length wig and carried two tablets of stone all night long.

That response brought a smile to everyone's face, but I had no idea where this questioning was leading. However, the responses had not hurt our case so far, and I decided to see where the questioning would take us.

But I moved my coffee mug between Linc and me just to be sure he was cautious.

Lara continued:

Q: Aside from the time at the Purim festival, have you ever worn a wig?

Linc saw my coffee mug move into position. His response was short.

A: No.

Continuing her questioning, Agent Martin changed the topic from Linc's hair to his mustache.

Q: How long have you worn that mustache, Mr. Shapiro?
A: At least ten years.
Q: May I...

She reached out and touched Linc's mustache. She ran her fingers, almost sensuously, through its thickness on both sides of his nose and then gently yet forcibly tugged at each end. She nodded at her colleague and returned to her seat next to Grattan.

As soon as she was seated, Grattan looked Linc straight in the eye and said:

"Mr. Shapiro, on behalf of the Federal Bureau of Investigation, I would like to extend the Bureau's—as well as our personal—apology for the anxiety and stress we have caused you over the last two days."

To say Linc and I were shocked at his words would be the understatement of the year. The feeling of shock was immediately replaced by feelings of joy and relief in my heart and I could only imagine how Linc felt.

Agent Grattan looked directly at me and continued, "We were focusing on a tree and not looking at the entire forest. There was, in fact, a green 1992 Oldsmobile Cutlass parked on Seventh Avenue and an FBI team had that vehicle under surveillance. At approximately 4:30 p.m., an individual approached that car and spoke to the driver. That individual then went to the rear window on the passenger's side and had a conversation with a person in the car. At the end of the conversation, the individual in the vehicle handed a folded manila envelope to the person he was speaking with.

"What was not considered in the information relayed

to my unit was the fact that Seventh Avenue at 4:35 p.m. has a lot of people walking down the street toward the subway station. Adding to the confusion was the fact that it was raining moderately heavy on Monday. A number of men on the street were wearing raincoats and hats since, as we all know, you cannot walk on crowded New York City streets with an umbrella without hitting other pedestrians. The bureau had a second surveillance team on Barrow and Bleecker Streets, and they received a radio transmission that a man wearing a tan raincoat and brown hat stopped by the car under surveillance and engaged in conversation with the subjects. This person was designated Target 2. A member of the surveillance team was directed to pick up and follow Target 2 when he got to the corner.

"George, you were also wearing a tan raincoat and a brown hat, like several people on the block. When you turned on Barrow, the second surveillance team followed you to the garage, but you are not the guy who stopped at the car.

"You were so adamant in your denials that you engaged in conversation with our Target 1 and were so forthcoming about an extremely personal matter that Lara and I started to have doubts if you were involved in this matter. When we left our meeting yesterday, we went directly to the agents who were conducting the surveillance and requested to see the photographic evidence in this case. We examined the photos. They are grainy, since a long camera lens was being used in rainy weather conditions. We were able to get a good look at Target 2 at the passenger side window. When Target 2 bent down to speak to the passenger in the car, he lifted up his hat. Target 2 had a full head of hair and was clean-shaven. I guess this is a long way of saying that the individual we were after got mixed up in the crowd, and the Bleecker Street surveillance team picked you up instead of the real target."

Linc and I were dumbfounded at the revelation.

We thought that Grattan was finished, but he continued.

"George, I want to assure you and your attorney that any discussions we had in these past two days will not be reflected in any FBI reports and what you did in New York City that day is strictly your business and that no one in this room can ever divulge it.

"Concerning the meeting we had yesterday … it never happened."

You can do such things in Matters Involving National Security.

Conclusion

I hope you enjoyed sitting in on and hearing my war stories. The 1948 movie *The Naked City* said it best: "There are eight million stories in the naked city."

Well, my friends Patrick, Frank and I don't have anywhere near eight million stories but when we get together, we definitely have our favorites, which we always seem to share. Our friendship goes back to 1971 when we first met working at the Nassau County Legal Aid Society. We became lifelong friends, even though we are very different. Frank is a renaissance man and a liberal. Patrick is an Irish Catholic and a conservative. Me, I am the Italian kid somewhere in the middle.

While we came from different backgrounds, we all shared the common values of helping people and seeing justice was done. Being lawyers gave us the opportunity to do what we loved. Each day, a different problem comes across your desk. Sometimes the phone rings with a person who is facing a traumatic personal problem on the other end. To fulfill your obligation as a lawyer, you have to supplement your knowledge of the law with empathy.

Just reflect on how clients feel when they call you from jail. They are embarrassed for themselves, their spouse and especially their children. They are scared of the court system and terrified of jail. Just the day or two they may have spent in the lock up before they made bail makes an indelible imprint on their brains. Being handcuffed, told where to sit or stand, where to walk, when to eat or sleep is just a small amount of the deprivation of freedom they have to bear and the stuff for nightmares that are no doubt in their future. The clank of a cell door closing echoes down a sterile hallway and is repeated over and over again in the hearer's mind. They have heard that a substantial number of prisoners have psychological problems and they fear for their safety. They need to learn fast the rules of prison life. The do's and don'ts. What to say or not. What to hear or not. They are told that an inmate was stabbed to death recently over a dispute with another inmate over a sandwich consisting of two slices of baloney and day-old white bread.

You are there on the worst days of their lives. You are the lifeboat in a storm that looks like it will drown them.

That's what being a criminal trial attorney is about, and I hope these nine stories gave you a peek at what goes on in the mind of a criminal trial attorney and those he works with to achieve justice.

Just as it is inscribed on the county courthouse,

"Justice is God's idea—Man's ideal."

And each day, you get the opportunity to strive for that lofty goal.

Acknowledgments

In this new world of independent publishing, there's a lot you have to do aside from putting words on paper. If you're like me and unable to type, the first thing you need to do is find a good soul that will take your scribblings and decipher them into a first draft. Then you need a friend who not only has a degree in English but also is not afraid to give you her honest, no-holds-barred opinion. (I find that real estate agents are best at this task.) From there, you have to impose upon a kid who you met over fifty years ago in your first law school class and who is, thankfully, a practicing trial attorney, to painstakingly go through your 250-page manuscript to check it for accuracy. Then it's off to another friend to review your grammar and syntax.

Thank you—Kay, Carolyn, Bobby and Barbara.

After you reach this stage, which for me took about two years, you need to reach out to the pros. Nora Gaskin Esthimer was an accidental find. In our first meeting, I was impressed with her honest and no-nonsense attitude when it came to developmental editing. We spent several rounds going back-and-forth on the manuscript, and she taught me more about writing than I could get from a college level course. Then it was off to Kelly Prelipp Lojk at Lojk Design for copyediting, book layout and design. Last, but not least, in this day and age you need a website to get the word out. Thanks to Sean Brosnan for creating and designing **gnacbooks.com**.

The saying goes that it takes a village, and it certainly has been true in this case. Without the help of these people who gave their time and expertise to this project, my dream would not have been transformed into reality.

A Favor, Please

I hope you enjoyed *You Can't Make This Stuff Up,* and I hope you will tell your friends who like good stories about the book.

As you may know, 50 percent of the profit of this book will go equally to two Cary, North Carolina, charitable organizations: Citizens Assisting Police's Christmas gift program for needy children and Nourishing Noggins, which provides food and other basic necessities to children at Mills Park Elementary. My profit is in the telling of these stories, in which I take great enjoyment.

You can help make these donations meaningful.
- Tell your friends about the book.
- Post comments on social media.
- Review the book on www.amazon.com and www.goodreads.com.
- Suggest the book to your reading group.

I have more stories to tell and look forward to
You Can't Make This Stuff Up, Vol. 2.

For more information, visit my web site
at **gnacbooks.com**

Till then, thanks for your help and God bless.
    – Gregg